OLD MAN
ON CAMPUS

by Barry J. Brownstein

DEDICATION

This book is dedicated to my family.

To my parents, Herbert and Sylvia, who valued education and channeled my brother Scott and me in that direction from my earliest memory. You probably were surprised just how often I went back to college. And, Mom, thanks for proofreading an early version of this manuscript. This book is dedicated to your memory.

To our children—Gary, Katie, and Daniel—and grandchildren—Patrick, Noah, Liam, Sanford Wolfe, and those who may follow—it is a special joy watching you grow. May you always follow your dreams, even if a few more years spool by along the way than you had planned.

And especially to my wife, Linda, mother of three, grandmother of four, and the most balanced person I know. Over the past forty-four years, you have encouraged and supported me, never flinching at the risks. You make my life possible. Your love, confidence, and encouragement brighten my days. May I always do the same for yours.

ACKNOWLEDGMENTS

A story involving my education would not be complete without thanking several groups of people...

I will always be indebted to the public school teachers who taught me all those years ago in Rome, New York, and Beltsville, Maryland. Whether our paths crossed at Garden Street School, Fort Stanwix Elementary, Staley Junior High, Rome Free Academy, or High Point High School: thank you. And thanks also to the instructors and professors at the University of Maryland, University of Michigan, Wright State University, Otterbein College, Franklin County Firefighters/Grant Medical Center EMS Education Program, Columbus State Community College, and Marietta College.

Much of medical education depends on preceptors who give students practical experience and training. I have been fortunate to have had many good ones over the years and cannot possibly mention all of them here. Of special note are Tina Quinn, who took a green EMT under her wing; Carla Blazier, who has made countless new paramedics comfortable in the field; and Dr. Michael Alexander, whose mix of compassion, expertise, and humor put me on the road to becoming a clinician. I am pictured with "Dr. A" on the back cover of this book. I am especially grateful to Dr. Manmohan Katapadi, my supervising physician, who continues to train me, trusts me to care for his patients, and encourages me to pay it forward by being a preceptor for others.

My gratitude goes out to all of the dedicated first responders I have had the good fortune to work with and learn from over the years—first at the Minerva Park Volunteer Fire Department and, later, at the Madison County Emergency Medical District. And thanks also to responders from neighboring departments and local law enforcement who worked so well together, even if we had never met before those sometimes frenetic, middle-of-the-night scenes. People passing through our districts did not know your names, but their lives were safer in your hands.

To the Marietta College Physician Assistant Class of 2006: thank you for accepting me into your midst and making my twenty-seven months with you so special.

Thanks to this book's project team at CreateSpace, who led me through the process of getting my story on paper.

And to my friends, you know who you are, some of you have moved on or passed away, but you will always remain in my heart. Your encouragement, humor, and support over the years have been deeply appreciated. You also have taught me one of the most valuable lessons: the core pleasure of life comes from those you get to meet along the way.

TABLE OF CONTENTS

CHAPTER 1

JOURNEYS

When you've parked the second car in the garage, and installed the hot tub, and skied in Colorado, and windsurfed in the Caribbean; when you've had your first love affair and your second and your third, the question will remain: where does the dream end for me?

—Mario Cuomo

Marietta College, Marietta, Ohio, June 21

We five members of Team George stand next to a large metal table holding our covered cadaver. We remove two sheets and expose George, who is still under a blue sheet saturated with pink embalming fluid. Carefully removing the blue sheet, we find an elderly man lying face down. He is going to be our teaching aid for the summer.

A chemical smell starts to build at our table. It's not overpowering at first, but, soon, eyes begin to water. "I've got to get some air," one of our teammates gasps as she moves quickly to the door. And I have to ask myself, how in the world did I end up here?

Westerville, Ohio, One Week Earlier

A neighbor on her early-morning walk pauses in front of our house while her two small dogs sniff the dew-laden grass around the mailbox. It's a typical morning on Autumn Tree Place, but not for me. I back the car out of the driveway and wave good-bye to Linda. She waves back from the same spot where we stood together on other days, watching with that unique mixture of excitement and sadness as each of our three children left home for college and the greater world beyond. Now, somehow, it's my turn, at age fifty-eight.

I've quit what will probably be the highest paying job of my life and filled my car with clothes and books. Forty years removed from my first freshman year, I'm leaving home again to go back to college—this time to become a physician assistant. I'll be living alone for the first time in my life while I train to become a "PA," the latest in a long line of new futures.

It's only a two-hour trip to Marietta, Ohio, but the journey to this day has been much longer. The first time I went to college, it was to become an aerospace engineer. That career path started early; one of my oldest memories is of Dad playfully chasing his three-year-old son through a field of propeller-driven P-51 fighter planes on a sunny afternoon.

With Dad, in my
ducking-under-airplane-wings stage.

Just outside of Rome, New York, Griffiss Air Force Base became a magical place for me. Aircraft were always overhead during the day, and the nightly sounds of engines being run up on the flight line floated in through my bedroom window.

Rome in the early 1950s was full of people who had recently been touched by war, and it often seemed like we weren't that far from another conflict. Kids everywhere were being taught to hide under their flimsy desks in case of nuclear war, but our town was special. Fighter pilots from Griffiss hunted for Russian bombers over the Canadian tundra while wearing orange flight suits so that rescue crews could spot them in the snow. Bomber crews on alert rode through town in specially marked trucks that could whisk them back to waiting aircraft if the not-so-unthinkable happened.

Surrounded by all this purposeful activity, I took it as a given that I was supposed to find something important to do with my life; not just striving to be rich and famous but to end up doing something worthy. I had no idea what that might be, and the search for a satisfactory answer would become a recurring theme in my life.

Though my parents had grown up in an era of limited options, they emphasized the importance of education and made sure that their kids studied hard. My younger brother, Scott, and I knew from an early age that our futures would somehow involve going to college, whatever that meant. Eventually we both went to the University of Maryland, near where our family had moved when Dad went to work for NASA.

I expect that my first day of PA school next week will be a major milestone, but nowhere near as life changing as was my first day at Maryland. Sitting next to me there in freshman English was Linda, a very pretty girl with a great sense of humor. Four years later, I graduated as an aerospace engineer, and, at an ROTC ceremony, Linda's father commissioned me as an air force second lieutenant. We were married a few weeks later. I knew from day one that I had married out of my league. I'm guessing Linda would say that her sense of humor has served her well through all the years since.

As young married life can do, the years flashed by quickly: graduate school in Ann Arbor, followed by active duty in Dayton. Our son Gary was born. I resigned from the air force but stayed on as a civilian while attending graduate school at night to study computer engineering. We bought our first house. Our daughter Katie was born. We moved to Westerville, a suburb of Columbus, when I took a job with a large research and development firm. Our son Daniel was born. Linda and I were thirty-five years old, and our nuclear family—The Original Five—was complete.

I sip my coffee and settle in for the drive to Marietta, a city of about 15,000 on the banks of the Ohio River. Wedged in between piles of belongings, I have to smile as I recall the activities of the past few weeks. The most obvious harbinger of change had been the steadily growing pile of supplies in our garage. Eventually it included a bed, computer gear, dishes, reference materials, office supplies, and a TV. Some friends even donated furniture left over from their children's college years. In yet another touch of irony, my octogenarian parents added to the loot when they insisted on buying their not-so-young son a new microwave oven for his college apartment. My father also loaned me his old stereo. Thanks, Dad; now if only I could find my old Beach Boys album.

Just yesterday, Linda and I loaded these provisions onto a rented truck and drove to an empty apartment in a newly rehabilitated warehouse about a mile from campus that will be my home for the next twelve months. Unlike our early marriage days when we moved to Michigan, this time we didn't have to manhandle a two-wheel U-Haul trailer to the steps of the apartment, nor did Linda wear a green bikini during the unloading process. Instead, definitely older—and presumably more resourceful—we asked our son Gary to meet us and help unload.

Driving toward Interstate 70 this morning, my car is just one drop in a river of commuters. Watching them drive to work, I feel the joy of finally starting out on an adventure after years of preparation. But I have some doubts too.

Twelve years ago, I launched myself as a self-employed project management consultant. I enjoyed the work and my clients, was paid very well, and the job gave me a great deal of freedom. Was I crazy to quit my job? Do I really have enough functioning brain cells left to complete a master's-level physician assistant program with students less than half my age? And how did I end up even wanting to do this now, at fifty-eight?

Like many young children, I had several early run-ins with medicine, usually involving the business end of a syringe full of something that burned. Running was a favorite mode of transportation, and I didn't always look where I was going. A year or two after my broken field run at the air base, I ran into our backyard picnic table. I picked myself up in a panic; I was breathing, but it still didn't feel like I was getting any air.

Somehow I found Mom, and—between the few words I could get out, a rapidly swelling torso, and some wild gestures—she understood that something was very wrong. The world was a different place in 1951. Rome didn't have an Emergency Medical Service, let alone 9-1-1. Soon I was being rushed to the hospital in a neighbor's car, going in and out of consciousness on the way.

I don't remember much after that until I awoke to find my parents in my hospital room. Brown rubber tubes ran from metal needles poking in my skin to a small white porcelain water bowl. A bubble would appear every second or so, and I watched bubbles for days.

I later learned that Dr. Frank H. Valone had manipulated a cartilage ring in my airway back into place, literally saving my life. Forever referred to by my family as "the bubble doctor," he would be invited to every major celebration in my life. When he retired some twenty years after our encounter at the hospital, we exchanged letters, and he described my near-death experience as if it were yesterday. Only then did I understand the degree to which I have been living on bonus time all these years.

With my brother, Scott,
recuperating from the
picnic table accident.

At age eleven, I began going to Camp Kingsley, a Boy Scout camp in the Adirondacks, in whose pine and birch forests I refined my reputation as a frequent casualty. My sojourn in camp was cut short one year when I sliced my foot with an axe while trying to chop down a small tree. Another year I was taken to a local physician and then returned to camp with a badly infected wound. A resident air force corpsman who took care of kids like me treated me daily for the rest of my stay. I'm sure I was his best customer.

Besides being aware of the medical profession, I got some early encouragement to consider medicine as a career. Mom's uncle Jessie, the physician who delivered me, was one of our few relatives to have gone to college. When we visited his family, my cousin Naomi showed me how to operate the centrifuge in his office.

Medicine did look interesting, but whatever idea I might have harbored about it as a career died abruptly at the 1958 New York State Fair. My family and the twelve-year-old version of me wandered into an eye-bank exhibit, complete with human corneas. For some reason, it horrified me, and my mind wouldn't process another thought for the rest of the day. Even now, just listening to a song that played on the radio on our way home from the fair still reminds me of just how unsettled I felt.

I drive east this morning through Zanesville, taking note of landmarks along what I expect will be a frequent route back and forth between school and home. I pass a McDonalds near the trip's midpoint and make a mental note. Someday I might want to grab a quick cup of coffee there to stay awake.

My backseat this morning is mostly full of books and clothes, but it also includes my blue emergency squad uniform. In addition to juggling the duties of student, husband, and father in the coming year, I also plan on continuing to take 9-1-1 calls two nights a month with a squad in central Ohio. In the hierarchy of improbable stories, the one about how a fifty-eight-year-old engineer ends up going to physician assistant school actually pales in comparison with the one about how a twelve-year-old traumatized by an eye-bank exhibit at the state fair ends up deciding to assist at auto accidents, shootings, and stabbings.

There is a Buddhist proverb that goes, "When the student is ready, the teacher will appear." Mine showed up a month or so after my thirty-eighth birthday.

Linda and I were running errands in Westerville when we blundered into the grand opening of St. Ann's Hospital. Linda wanted to take the tour, and, as usual, I didn't. Still, we went (when you've married out of your league, you know that you need to go that extra mile every now and then). We came to a volunteer sign-up table at the end of the tour, and, with some more of Linda's encouragement, I signed up.

I thought the hospital might take advantage of my technical skills, but instead I was assigned to the emergency room. It was an unsettling thought, even decades after the infamous eye-bank episode. "Please give it a try, " the interviewer pleaded. "Very few men have signed up as volunteers, and we really want to put one in the ER in case they need some muscle."

Now, no one has ever mistaken me for hired muscle. I'm guessing she also didn't know about how I stepped on my own track spikes in high school.

What started out as a tentative, Monday-evening experiment quickly became a serendipitous, life-changing experience. The hospital had sorely underestimated the demand for emergency services, and volunteers were pressed into service in unpredictable ways. I searched for pliers to cut fish-hooks, filled ice bags, got warm blankets for patients in shock, and retrieved sterile surgical kits from central supply. I calmed some patients and pulled traction on others during procedures. I also made beds and cleaned blood off the floor. Even helping in small ways gave me more pleasure than any job I had ever had.

During moments when life in the ER went quiet, I would sit and talk with the staff. After a while, physicians started to involve me more in patient care, such as having me hold wound edges while they sutured. After two years of volunteering, I came across a poster announcing an emergency-medical-technician course. Carole, a nurse who had befriended me, suggested that I give it a try.

Our nuclear family when I blundered into medicine.
From left: Katie, me, Linda, Daniel, and Gary.

I'm now forty miles from Marietta, near Cambridge, just turning south on Interstate 77 for the final leg to the Ohio River. I change lanes to let an ambulance go by, its lights flashing. After twenty years in EMS, I can picture its crew at their stations, preparing for what they might find at the scene, carefully watching the cars around them, and getting aggravated when drivers don't get out of the way quickly enough.

The EMT Basic class Carole had recommended was held at a fire department about half an hour from home. For two nights each week—and with classmates half my age—we covered the essentials of prehospital trauma and emergency medical care. We learned how to bandage injuries, splint broken bones, and deliver babies. We rolled each other around on gurneys so we could experience life from the patient's perspective. We went to a junkyard and cut into cars with the Jaws of Life.

There were also the pranks one might expect from eighteen-year-old kids, but little did I realize then how essential a good sense of humor would be for one's sanity in the world of EMS. One evening we practiced immobilizing a trauma patient on a backboard, using our classmate Mike as a guinea pig. Then we left him helplessly propped up against a dumpster and went back inside the station.

When we graduated, another nurse in the ER steered me to a local volunteer fire department. Soon, in addition to my day job, I was riding occasional nights and weekends as a newly minted EMT with the Minerva Park Volunteer Fire Department. We served a village of a few hundred homes that, years earlier, had started the department with a single fire engine. Old-timers told us about being at home and responding to the sound of a pole-mounted siren, along with stories of unfortunate equipment breakdowns on their way to fire scenes.

By the time I arrived, Minerva Park Fire had long since disposed of its engine and contracted for fire protection from Columbus, which had grown to virtually surround it. All that remained of the old department was a volunteer EMS unit (the last such unit in the county) founded 20 years earlier by several women in the village. At the time, a newspaper article—presumably using acceptable language of the day—described it as the "squaw squad." As more women entered careers outside the home, the department began depending on male and female volunteers from across the metropolitan area. By the time I joined, only one of the original women remained.

Soon I was riding with the squad for up to a hundred hours a month, mostly evenings and weekends, while keeping my demanding day job and trying to be a good father and husband. Most of our members were young, many with low-paying jobs they were using to survive until they could get on with paying fire departments. Those of us who were older took part because it added something to our lives that we couldn't quite explain; we certainly weren't there for the money. Instead, we had given up our free time for the moment we would hear: "Squad 119, for Columbus, with Engine 24, injured person, 1234 Morse Road, cross street Tamarack, time out: 2236..."

Once on scene, we would find one or more patients, along with distraught family or curious bystanders. Depending on the nature of the call, we might be alone or joined by the police, an engine company, or another

EMS unit. The unfolding nature of events at a scene taught us to think fast, focus on the basics, be willing to improvise, and work closely with others.

Many incidents would turn out to be minor and, sometimes, even humorous. The "person trapped" was a man who was moving a sofa bed when it suddenly sprang open and trapped him in a hallway. The "dead body in the lake" turned out to be an unfortunate raccoon. A middle-of-the-night "injured child" call came from two young parents who were terrified because their child had just turned one that day and still hadn't started to walk.

But other calls did involve life and death emergencies. A car fleeing the police slammed into a gas station, an ejected passenger trapped and paralyzed under the vehicle. A nephew found his aunt's lifeless body lying next to her bed. Guarded by a policewoman with a cocked shotgun, we worked on a young man with a bullet in his chest while a melee went on around us. A young woman returning from class was cut off in traffic, lost control, and struck a car containing a father and his two sons on their way to a baseball game.

Heart attacks, strokes, motorcycle accidents, suicides: sometimes I would start an IV, apply oxygen, do CPR, reassure the patient, or bandage a wound. Sometimes I just ran for equipment or helped move the patient to a waiting helicopter, rotors still turning, in a deserted parking lot in the middle of the night. And sometimes I just tried to help the family, making an appearance at what would be just the beginning of their own unique nightmare.

My overloaded car is now entering the hilly terrain of Appalachian Ohio, about twenty miles north of Marietta. We have lived in Ohio for twenty-seven years, and I had never made this trip until I started looking into nearby colleges with physician assistant programs. More to the point, I had no knowledge of the PA profession whatsoever until an EMT on our squad asked me for a letter of recommendation.

Few of the younger members of the squad stayed for very long. For most, it was a place to discover who you were and gain experience before finding a paying job elsewhere. After I became assistant chief, one pleasant new duty involved writing letters of recommendation. Scott, a young EMT, asked for one so that he could apply for a physician assistant program near Dayton. He told me that PAs are "mid-level providers," between physicians and nurses, licensed to practice medicine with physician supervision. While supervision rules differ from state to state and practice to practice, PAs work one on one with patients in virtually every medical specialty.

A few years later, I left the squad and soon found myself in something of a midlife enthusiasm slump. While work was going well, I was starting to feel old and stale. I had long since learned that being dissatisfied isn't all bad, especially if it spurs you on to do something productive. In this instance, it got me to track Scott down and find out how his life as a physician assistant had turned out. I found him working in an emergency room in Zanesville, enthusiastic and obviously enjoying himself. After going back to shadow him at work for a day, I began thinking about becoming a PA myself.

As I saw it, becoming a PA had three advantages. First, it was a good combination of science and people, the two elements of my world that I was most interested in. Second, it was a worthy job. I had learned from my years in EMS that helping people gave me a great sense of satisfaction. Third, it seemed doable for someone my age. Not counting prerequisite courses, the two-plus years of training seemed reasonable compared to the decade or so that it could take to become a physician.

I made two decisions over the next few months. The first was to get back into EMS. Through a friend and former EMS instructor, Barb D'Onofrio, I got connected with the Madison County Emergency Medical District and began working there a few nights each month. It felt good to be back in EMS. The second decision was to start taking the prerequisites I would need for PA school.

Sifting through our family's deluge of junk mail, I came across an announcement for an organic chemistry night class at nearby Otterbein College. Even though I hadn't taken a college course in twenty years, it seemed as good a place to start as any. It proved to be a challenge. Once again, I was the oldest student and the one furthest removed from his or her last college course. I was fortunate to be in a small class with helpful classmates, especially Yadwiga, a professional chemist trained in Poland who was pursuing an American degree. I would later discover another connection to Yadwiga.

After my year at Otterbein, I took the rest of my prerequisites at night at Columbus State Community College. If you ever feel your enthusiasm for life waning, consider sitting in on a community college night class and meeting some of the students. You'll find that you aren't the only one there with a dream.

It took several years of taking one class at a time to finish the prerequisites. Not quite ready to retire and leave my family, I took a year off along the way to go to paramedic school at night. Once again, I was the old guy in a room full of people my children's age, at least until a gray-haired, retired dentist came in and sat down beside me.

As it turned out, Fred was also planning to go to PA school and was a year ahead of me in preparation. We enjoyed our training and became friends. Besides going to two or three classes each week, we had hundreds of hours of clinical rotations. While in our ER rotation, Fred and I would wade into whatever case was going on like we belonged. Fred's motto was, "We're too old to ask for permission!" Not a bad strategy. All that year, Fred encouraged me to overcome my remaining doubts, finish my last year of prerequisites, and just go to PA school. By the time we graduated as paramedics, I had long since agreed with him.

I was not certain how PA programs would look on a prospective student quite so long in the tooth. I started exploring some of the closer schools. I was making a motel reservation one night while on duty at the squad bay, and Carla Blazer, the lieutenant on our shift, overheard me asking if they had an AARP rate. She started laughing, adding, "You should ask if the school has an AARP discount!"

One school I investigated was the new PA program at Marietta College. Jen, another paramedic on our squad, was also interested in their program. One pleasant summer day, Linda, and I made the kind of college visit we'd taken with our children not so many years before, but with Jen in tow this time. Our arrival at the college initially led to some confusion. We had to make it clear to the academic coordinator that Linda and I weren't two parents taking their daughter on a college trip; Linda was accompanying not one, but two prospective students. As we toured the classroom building, we looked in on a class where students were intently studying skulls. I could picture myself in there with them.

Marietta College's program had the advantage of letting me move back home after my first twelve months and then commute to clinical rotations in the metropolitan Columbus area for the remainder of the program. Katie and her husband Tom had just told us that we would soon be grandparents, so minimizing my time away from home had become even more of a priority.

After I was accepted, I came back to meet my twenty-five-year-old *big brother* in the class just ahead of mine. Over sandwiches at the Third Street Deli, he shared his insight about what I could expect. Clearly I should come prepared to work.

In retrospect, the decision seven years ago to take that first night class wasn't really such a big step; I still went to work the next day. In terms of my mental outlook though, it was huge. I was finally on the path that eventually brought me here, to the outskirts of Marietta.

CHAPTER 2

BASE CAMP MARIETTA

With Linda on moving day.

I t's late morning by the time I pull up to the IGA grocery at the edge of town. In the vernacular of my old air force buddies, I'm a "class B bachelor on TDY"—living away from my wife while on temporary duty. And, as a new, somewhat-older-than-usual college student, I'm ready to stock up on the necessities of the solitary life I've never experienced before.

I move briskly around the store, tossing condiments, vegetables, canned goods, and beverages into my cart. Up to now, I've never had to cook for myself for an extended period. While I can cook, I'm not that good at it, to be honest. I took over the job—albeit briefly—when Daniel was born. It's the only job I've ever been fired from, and by my own family, no less. In their defense, my dinners did take hours to make, and, in spite of an elaborate gourmet cookbook I bought especially for the occasion, they really weren't worth the wait.

I'm not usually patient enough to cook when I'm hungry and alone, which will probably happen a lot this year. The advent of more imaginative prepared foods has helped. I'm always on the lookout for new, easy-to-make meals, and there's one over there.

The new product: precooked pasta and sauce that doesn't even need refrigeration. Picking up the package and reading the directions, I note that it's "a complete serving" of spaghetti, just needing a scant few minutes in my new microwave before it bursts on the scene as a "delicious dinner." Truthfully, it doesn't look all that appetizing, lying there, waxy-looking, behind the clear plastic wrap. I decide to buy it anyway to keep around for emergencies. Emergencies like running out of fresh food or ideas about what one really does to convert fresh food into dinner.

I pull into the lot behind my apartment and park at my back door. It's a small building with two small stores and seven apartments. It's a quiet early summer afternoon. Mine is the only car in the lot, and apparently mine is the only apartment currently rented. I unlock the door and step into my new world.

Even with yesterday's cargo, the apartment still feels empty. The rooms are large, each with just a few pieces of furniture. Being alone today makes the place seem even emptier. The century-old building was constructed as an apartment, later converted to a warehouse, and now it has become an apartment again. Some of the old charm has been retained: my new study has glass doors at either end, and every room has a high ceiling, wide wooden moldings, and a transom over its doorway.

In spite of this being the middle unit on the first floor of a two-story building, somehow there are skylights in the bathroom and study. One of these days, I hope to find out how that was done. When viewed from the rear, the building is scalloped between every second unit, so I have windows on three sides.

I quickly unload the car. Finding a place for the groceries is easy; the kitchen is at least as large as the one I left this morning. I guess people ate well a century ago. Clothes, on the other hand, must have been in short supply. There are only two closets, if you can call them that. One is a small, triangular affair in my bedroom, with just enough space to hang a pair of jeans from one hook and pajamas from the other. My study has a closet capable of holding about two feet of hanging clothes. What I brought today just fits, so I'll have to swap wardrobes in and out as my needs change.

Lieutenant Carla Blazer was my secret Santa at our squad's Christmas party last year. With great fanfare, she gave me some gifts she thought would be especially appropriate for someone about to live alone for the first time. Many of her gifts—refrigerator containers for leftovers, a laundry basket, and dish towels—find new homes here.

It doesn't take long to get everything put away, and, once again, the place falls silent. I feel an overwhelming urge to make this feel more like home, so I put a small leprechaun statue and a Swarovski crystal bear in the window over my kitchen sink. Both have nearly identical twins sitting in our kitchen window back home. The continuity, minor though it may be, is comforting.

While I would very much like to explore the town, I have to wait for the telephone installer and the cable TV guy. Both show up promptly. The cable guy turns out to be a gruff-spoken man about my age. I follow him around the apartment as he does his work because I'm mildly interested, and I really don't have anything else to do.

"So," I say, trying to break the ice. "You must have an interesting job, seeing new homes and new technology."

"I hate this job!" he retorts. "And, *thank God*, this is my last week."

"What are you going to do?" I ask.

"I'm retiring," he responds. "And what do you do?"

"I've retired, and I'm here to go to college."

"Why the *hell* would anyone want to do that?" he sputters.

"Well," I start. "I've wanted to be a physician assistant for a while now, and I finally have a chance to give it a try."

"You've got to be crazy to retire just to get another job!"

I hope this guy doesn't know something that I don't. Once he finishes his work and leaves with his personal cloud of gloom, I survey my new world. I spend some time setting up my computer and the old stereo my father lent me, as well as hanging a shade in my bedroom window. When I'm through, not only can I watch TV if I want to, but I can also get on the Internet and send messages to my family.

The apartment is now functional and, between the stereo and the TV, I can make some noise to break the otherwise unrelenting silence. Still, it doesn't feel much like home. It's also devoid of a few critical modern necessities, such as toilet paper. I make the first of what I expect will be many trips to Walmart.

Among other prizes, today's retail foraging yields photo paper for my computer printer and a number of picture frames in assorted sizes. I review pictures stored on my hard drive and pick out several to print, mount, and hang. Some are from the trip to Ireland that Linda and I took after my retirement. Others are of family and friends. This takes hours, but, when I finish hanging the pictures, it finally feels like I actually live here.

I make dinner when it gets dark. No, not the shelf-stable spaghetti. I uncap a beer from the IGA, turn on the TV, sit down on my friend Al's beat-up old yellow leather chair, and eat the first meal I've ever had while living on my own. The new picture on a nearby wall is comforting. It's of Linda and me dining outside with old air force friends at a reunion in Telluride two years ago. Fortunately, it doesn't show the nude cyclists who were riding by. I smile, recalling our discussions that day about how most people don't really look all that good biking in the nude.

So, like a space probe sent to another world, I've landed safely. More explorations tomorrow, but, for now, this is Base Camp Marietta signing off.

Bachelor fridge, day 1.

Opening my eyes the next morning, it takes a minute to remember where I am and that I don't have a job to go to today. Ah, but I do. I'll be spending the summer here in what sounds like a gross anatomy boot camp, and I have to spend most of the day studying its orientation materials. I took anatomy as part of my prerequisites, but, from the sound of it, that doesn't hold a candle to what's coming up.

Driving back later from another brief, mind-clearing trip to Walmart, I meet a young man going into the apartment next to mine. After twenty-four hours in town, I've finally met someone to talk to.

Bruce and I decide to go to dinner at a local Mexican restaurant, where we exchange information about our situations over some tasty food and a few beers. He is a newly minted PhD who has just joined the college's faculty. His wife is from Kazakhstan and stills lives in Athens, about an hour away. For the moment, we're both class B bachelors and the only renters in our building. We pool our scant knowledge of the town. My sole contribution is to tell him where the post office is. Other than the IGA, Walmart, and the post office, I haven't seen much yet.

Late the following morning, I finish my anatomy homework. It's finally time to leave the mother ship and start exploring the town on foot. I step out the back door into the humid, eighty-five-degree day. My first destination is the campus, about a mile east of my apartment.

My end of town is made up mostly of older homes, some subdivided into flats for student rentals. Walking down tree-lined Fourth Street toward campus, I pass homes with broad, open front porches and children out front playing on the sidewalk. Adults and children invariably say "hi" as I pass, sometimes before I can get my own greeting out. Marietta seems like a friendly place so far, aside from the cable guy.

Just beyond my neighborhood, I pass an intersection with churches on opposite corners of the street and then a senior center. People not that much older than me are getting into a van for an outing somewhere. Farther on, down a long hill toward the college, Fourth Street is lined with large, old mansions. I pass the home of Charles Dawes, Calvin Coolidge's vice president and a Marietta College graduate. A lawyer who died at the Battle of Antietam owned another. Nearing the base of the hill, I pass a funeral home and the county sheriff's office before reaching the edge of campus.

Marietta College is not especially large: in the direction I'm walking, it's just two blocks long and about four blocks wide. I enter the campus at a brick gate flanked by flower gardens and then continue onto a grassy area dotted with large trees. Many of the stately buildings line a central brick walkway. I stroll the grounds, wondering what my year inside these buildings will be like.

After leaving the campus, my next stop is downtown, at the confluence of the Ohio and Muskingum Rivers. A plaque announces this as the spot where General Lafayette came ashore during a goodwill tour of the West in the early 1800s. The riverfront still conjures up images of what it must have been like here when stern-wheelers plied these waters during the nineteenth century. Today the river is quiet, except for occasional tugs pushing strings of coal barges downstream.

Marietta's downtown projects a different image; it looks to be fighting a valiant battle just to survive. Numerous stores are closed or in the process of closing, and one stretch of storefronts remains boarded up from a fire that took place a few years ago. But there is life here too, in the form of busy antique shops, historical markers, a nice river walk along the Ohio, and numerous restaurants. I also find a community theater with a marquee announcing a play opening in a few days.

I stop by the Third Street Deli for a late lunch on my way home. A friendly lady behind the counter pegs me as new in town and strikes up a conversation. Like our son Daniel, her son also works at a radio station in Columbus. She's surprised to learn why I'm in town. I seem to be getting that a lot.

I start Thursday by driving to the closest mall, which is thirty minutes away in Parkersburg. I want to buy a book to read for fun—hopefully there will still be time for that in my new world. Back at the apartment, I decide to explore the two stores at the end of my building.

I walk into a wedding planning shop and meet Alisha, one of the two, twenty-something roommates who run the place, along with the combination photography/tuxedo rental business next door. She is enthusiastic as she describes their business model, which is to do everything associated with a wedding, except for the food. I admire her energy and wish them well. Starting your own business isn't easy.

I relax for the rest of the evening and start reading my new book. I now have a basic knowledge of Marietta, with the notable exception of what will be going on inside those college buildings. But orientation starts in the morning, so, by this time tomorrow, I'll have met the people I'll be spending the next two years with.

CHAPTER 3

FRESHMAN AGAIN

Marietta, Friday, June 18

For the first time since I've moved here, the clock radio wakes me up. My days of idleness in the River City are over; we'll be in orientation all day today and tomorrow. I open my eyes, and the first thing I see is the old, wrinkled, gold-and-black cap with a small bill hanging on my bedpost.

I rediscovered my freshman beanie in our basement this spring and brought it here with me as something of a talisman. I got it forty years ago during orientation week at the University of Maryland. I still have pictures of my high school friend Bruce Arrett and me wearing our beanies and smiling in the summer sun. I also remember our orientation group sitting together in the cavernous field house while someone shouted at us from the floor below.

"Look to your right! Now, look to your left! Only one of you three will graduate!"

It would make the memory complete if he had called us maggots. I don't think he did, but you get the picture.

This time out, I walk into a conference room dressed in the only suit my tiny closet holds and wonder what the graduation statistics will be like here. I find a dozen or so well-dressed young people. My first thought: I hope they don't mistake me for a teacher. They don't seem to, and no one gasps at me. So far so good.

Bruce Arrett, with freshman beanie, 1964.

Some stragglers follow me in, bringing our total to twenty. We exchange names, hometowns, and basic personal information while we wait for someone in authority to show up. With the exception of three former Marietta undergrads who seem to know each other and two students who were randomly matched as roommates, no one seems to know anyone else.

I recognize Seren from our interviews in February. He's a friendly, athletic guy from Florida, with family nearby in southeastern Ohio. Michelle is the youngest in our class; she just turned twenty-one. She went to school in Missouri and has a boyfriend back home. I get the impression that she feels Marietta is in the middle of nowhere.

Kim is a vivacious woman from Cincinnati who went to college in Virginia. She spent the past year working as an EMT to gain experience for the program. She has a humorous, easygoing style and already seems like great fun to talk to.

We have a Jen here too, but not the same one who accompanied Linda and me here last summer. She's an intelligent, dark-haired woman from northern Ohio. Jen last lived in Nashville, where the local UPS man introduced her to her fiancé. She is quiet and has an easy smile.

Kevin is one of three former Marietta students. An athletic training student as an undergraduate, he played on the Marietta football team. Kevin is an outgoing guy and is engaged to a student teacher in Columbus.

After a few minutes, a short, friendly woman with a strong New England accent enters and introduces herself. She is Dr. Gloria Stewart, director of the PA program and our host. We all quickly end up on a first name basis, including Gloria. She begins by telling us about ourselves. Most of our class is right out of college, and, other than me, no one is older than twenty-nine. Our class's average age is only twenty-five, even with me vigorously pulling up my end of the curve.

Our group is composed of seven men and fourteen women, including a woman from the class ahead of us who has decided to take another year to graduate. She has already taken anatomy, so she won't be joining us until the fall. One of our original classmates withdrew from the program just a few days ago, and a replacement pulled from the waiting list virtually at the last moment is on his way, driving across the country from Colorado.

We're deep into filling out paperwork when the cross-country straggler finally arrives. Stan is an athletic Asian man in his late twenties who has been driving night and day. Unlike the rest of us, he's still wearing his driving outfit of shorts and a Pac-Man T-shirt. He's not at all self-conscious about being late or dressed differently, and I like him already.

I walk over and introduce myself during a break. Stan looks familiar and we discover that he also was in the same interview group this winter with Seren and me. He tells me the story of how he got here.

Stan had been wait-listed for PA school and had gone on with his life in Colorado. Having recently graduated from college, he was at a crossroad in his life and had applied for more than one possible career. He had been accepted by the Phoenix policy academy and was actually loading his car for the twelve-hour trip when he got the call from Marietta. He changed his mind on the spot and left to come here instead. Now he's staying in an empty dorm until he can make other living arrangements. In spite of changing his career and compass direction on the fly, Stan projects an easy air of inner calm.

Later, we meet our instructors, fill out more paperwork, and get formal portraits taken. I loan Stan my tie for his picture, while another classmate closer to his size lends him a shirt and coat.

Gloria then takes us on a tour. The main lecture room, our home for the next twelve months, seats twenty-two and is equipped with an overhead projection system for viewing PowerPoint lectures. There's a refrigerator at the back of the room for our lunches. It also will hold snacks that we'll buy as a group and then sell to each other, placing the proceeds in a ceramic piggy bank on top of the fridge. Nearby are mailboxes the program will use to give us assignments and handouts.

The clinical room is next door. It's a large, open room with padded benches in the center for our physical examination and splinting classes. Arranged around three of the walls are assigned study carrels, each with a desk and a locking cabinet. On the fourth wall are entrances to three small exam rooms.

Each exam room is equipped with what you'd probably find in your doctor's office, including an examination table, sink, and chrome shelves holding glass jars of gauze and other supplies. Colorful posters of various body systems are on the walls, along with multiple examination tools. Each room also has a TV camera and microphone mounted high on one wall so that our examinations can be recorded and critiqued by our instructors.

The computer lab is across the hall, with enough desktop computers for each of us. We'll be taking virtually all of our tests here to help prepare for our national boards—also taken by computer—in two and a half years.

The distance-learning room is on the floor below. It has a similar look to our classroom, except for a large television with a videoconference hookup so we can receive lectures from off-campus professors.

I sit next to Jan during lunch in the classroom. A young, dark-haired woman from the rural area just north of Marietta, she's a newlywed, making her one of only three of us who are married. After graduating from Marietta with an athletic training degree, she went to Marshall University for a master's degree in cardiac rehabilitation.

After lunch, we take a tour of Marietta General Hospital, which is just across the street from my apartment. As we jockey through its hallways, I meet Aaron, a tall, friendly midwesterner from Iowa. The third married member of our class, Aaron was a high school science teacher for several years before coming here. He and his wife, Liz, own a condo on the outskirts of town, just across the road from the Ohio River. Liz is able to telecommute to her job in Iowa.

Returning to the classroom after the tour, we meet Mr. B, as he wants to be called, a retired funeral director and manager of our cadaver lab. Mr. B is more like what I remember from my original freshman orientation, and he proceeds to put the fear of God in us. If he had a starched khaki uniform and a drill instructor's hat, the image would be complete.

"Any day you don't study—*including* Sundays—you *will* fall behind," he tells us gruffly. "This is a *total* immersion course. You will have *only* nine weeks to do what med students have *many* months for."

22

We're now free for the day, but, with Mr. B's warning still echoing in her ears, one of the women rushes home to study. Presumably it's out of fear of falling even a few hours behind those anonymous med students who have all that extra time to burn. Four of us decide to throw caution to the wind and go out to dinner.

"Do you think that guy was serious?" asks a dinner companion.

"My cousin goes to medical school," replies another. "They get a big packet of stuff to memorize every week in anatomy. It sounds like we're going to do the same thing, but in way less time."

"Oh well," says a third, taking a sip of his beer. "We're here. I'm just going to take it a day at a time."

I reflect on the day during my walk home after dinner in the warmth of an early summer evening. The adventure is finally under way. I do plan to take school seriously; it took a lot to get here, and there is still a heavy price to be paid, including a year away from my family. On the other hand, there have been times in my life when I was too goal-oriented. By only focusing on preparing for some future day, there have been times I missed out on some of the joy hidden in the day at hand. I don't want that to happen here.

By the time I unlock my back door, I have come to realize that I have three goals for this year. The first is to honor all these years of preparation by completing the program successfully. The second is to stay connected with my family and our friends. And the third is to reexperience the life of a college student, at least to the extent that a fifty-eight-year-old guy can go back in time.

Orientation continues on Saturday. After being given keys that provide twenty-four-hour access to the building, Gloria leads us downstairs for our first visit to the gross anatomy lab. Unlike other labs nearby, this one has blank sheets of poster board on the windows that block any view of the interior. Gloria unlocks the door, shares the combination, and ushers us inside.

We find five, large, empty, metal tables, each with a tray at one end and a lamp at the other. There is a list of names on each table, indicating the team of students who will be working there. We'll spend the rest of the summer with those teams, dissecting the cadavers that will be on the tables Monday, when school starts.

The college has never had a cadaver lab before. The two classes ahead of us were bused to the medical school at Ohio University, a two-hour round-trip. Our lives will be better without the lost commuting time. Though the college's resistance to having its own lab has been overcome, we learn there are some rules that we'll have to follow.

The first rule is never come to the lab alone; for safety, a buddy system is to be used. The second rule is never to let anyone into the lab who is not in our class. We are warned that failure to abide by this rule could lead to our dismissal. Gloria also suggests that we be vague if students outside of the program ask what goes on in our lab. Between the cipher lock, blank poster board, and security measures, I'm starting to feel like I'll be working in a classified government lab.

Orientation now over, we have a class picnic with our families. Linda has driven in for the occasion and gets the chance to meet the faculty, my classmates, and their parents. I expected to be older than all of my classmates (even our two older children would have that distinction if they were here instead of me), but, as we move around the room, I begin to realize that I'm also older than most of the parents.

After the picnic, Linda and I follow each other back to Westerville, where Gary, Daniel, Katie, and her husband, Tom, join us for brunch on Sunday. There is a lot to celebrate, including Daniel's twenty-third birthday and Father's Day.

When the kids leave, Linda and I—and Skyler, our yellow Labrador retriever—walk to a store and pick up some computer supplies that I couldn't find in Marietta. Then it's time for me to leave for my first real week of school. This produces an odd blend of the sadness associated with leaving and the anticipation of what is just ahead. I expect this too will become more familiar with time.

I stop at Trader Joe's on my way out of town, filling an ice chest with frozen meals for my nearly empty fridge. Two hours later, I walk into the apartment and unload, feeling a bit like a member of a Space Shuttle crew arriving at the International Space Station. I put my now-empty ice chest and recycling in an unused front entryway, whose doors at either end even remind me of an air lock. Katie's Fathers' Day gift was a bonsai tree, and it finds a home in the kitchen window. It's my only living companion here—I hope.

This isn't exactly the Lewis and Clark expedition, but my logistics here are surprisingly complex. I'll mostly eat what I can buy locally, but drinking water is a sensitive subject. We're in a swath of Ohio and West Virginia suspected of having contaminated ground water from a local chemical factory. I don't drink the tap water, and I already don't like the taste of the local bottled water. For the rest of my stay, in addition to my Trader Joe rations, I'll be bringing two-and-a-half-gallon water containers from a grocery in Westerville. When I go home, it will be with empty containers for curbside recycling, along with my dirty laundry.

It's time to take a look at our finances before the adventure starts in earnest tomorrow morning. We've been saving for this for quite a while, and my parents generously gave us some money a few years ago to help out. To commemorate their having done the same thing when each of their six grandchildren went to college, we once gave them a plaque with each graduation picture on it. When I finish this program, I'll have that plaque redone and add my picture.

My spreadsheet shows that we'll need to find some new money in about eighteen months. My parents continue to offer to help, which I really appreciate, but fifty-eight seems more than old enough for us to do the heavy lifting on our own. We'll either draw on our home equity loan or my 401(k). I'll review our finances monthly, and, for the moment, we're good to go. The financial review complete and the apartment stocked and ready, I take my shiny new key and walk to campus, where I watch a video in the empty classroom about tomorrow's rite of passage: the start of gross anatomy.

CHAPTER 4

TEAM GEORGE

Marietta, Monday, June 21

I'm up early for the first real day of school, dressed in my summer uniform of jeans, collared knit shirt, and comfortable shoes. I make a sack lunch of a peanut butter sandwich, an apple, some baby carrots, and a protein drink. Then, grabbing my copy of *Grant's Dissector* and our anatomy textbook, I'm out the door for the twenty-minute walk to campus. I have a photo at home Mom took on my first day of school in kindergarten. This time, though, I'm not wearing two-tone leather saddle shoes, and I don't think Mom is going to be hiding at various spots along the way to make sure I get there safely.

Three steps out into the warm morning and I realize that I've forgotten my lab outfit. We've been warned that whatever we wear to anatomy lab will pick up a preservative smell that mere laundry detergent can't touch. My disposable duds include an old pair of pants, a beat-up belt, discolored sneakers, and a shirt commemorating a customer's project from my previous life as a consultant. I package it all in an airtight garbage bag, and, finally, I'm ready to go.

I walk into a classroom full of people I barely know, so it really doesn't matter where I sit. Unlike my first day of college forty years ago, I'm not especially driven to find a pretty girl to sit next to. After all, this class B bachelor stuff only takes you so far. I'm feeling a little out of place, not so different from the first day of paramedic school. Probably not so different from the first day of kindergarten either, if I could remember what my class-mates back then thought of those two-tone shoes. I randomly pick an open seat in the front row, not realizing that this has just become my permanent spot at Marietta College.

First day of school, 1951.

I strike up a conversation with Hannah, a short woman with curly black hair who is sitting next to me. She has lived in Marietta for some time, owns her own home, and worked at a medical job across the river in West Virginia before starting school. When she decided to become a PA, this was the only school she applied to. "It was Marietta or nothing," she says. I find out that, at twenty-nine, she's the second oldest student in our class (just a few months younger than our daughter Katie).

Sitting nearby is Sylvia, a young woman from Alaska. She's the daughter of a fishing boat captain. When she was born, word of the event was transmitted from ship to ship so that it could reach her father. Her birthday was just a few days ago, on June 18. "So, you were born on a Thursday?" I ask. She gives me a startled look, as if she's just met Dustin Hoffman's savant character in *Rain Man*.

"I didn't figure that out in my head," I add quickly. "You just were born the day before my son Daniel."

Our program's academic coordinator enters, greets the class, and breaks the ice by telling us a little about himself. A balding man with a large mustache, Tim retired from the air force. He teaches here and also works one day each week as a PA at a local infectious disease clinic. One of his hobbies is acting in a local amateur theater company.

Tim explains that, in addition to our gross anatomy boot camp, we'll have two less intense courses this summer. The first is medical terminology, which will be self-taught, with weekly computerized exams. The second is radiology, which Tim will teach. It will progress through the body in the same sequence as our anatomy class.

After Tim has been talking for a few minutes, Stan comes in quietly and takes the empty seat on my left. He is already earning a reputation for getting places just a little later than everybody else. During a break, he tells me that he's still living in the dorm but is on the hunt for his own apartment.

Anatomy gets under way with an introduction from Mary Kay, our lead instructor from Ohio University. She'll be making the drive to Marietta three days a week and apparently today will be typical of our pace. We'll start out with a lecture, followed by a chance to change clothes, and then it's a full day of dissection in the lab, with one break for lunch. Mary Kay echoes Mr. B's warning: we'll be covering essentially the same material as a medical school class would, but in considerably less time, so don't fall behind.

Preliminaries behind us at last, she launches into a lecture on the anatomy of the spine. The material is very detailed and logical, but I feel like a nonswimmer getting a poolside lecture on how to swim. The instructions make sense, but soon I'll be in the deep end of a cold pool, thrashing around and trying to stay afloat. I've seen a century-old picture of my great-uncle Jessie and his medical school dissection team arrayed around their cadaver. In just a few minutes, that'll be me.

We scatter to find places to change clothes and then walk as a group down a floor to the lab. I'm dressed in the outfit from my garbage bag. Kim is wearing a Longhorn Steak House shirt, probably from a part-time job during school. Some people are wearing scrubs. We walk single file into the large, well-lit, and—at least for the moment—well-ventilated lab.

Mary Kay and Mr. B meet us inside. From his tone of voice, it's clear that Mr. B views this lab as his domain. We follow his orders, take lab coats from the rack, put on rubber gloves, and walk to our assigned tables.

I'm in a group of five students assembled around a table in the far-right corner of the room. In front of us, face down under a white sheet, is our cadaver. A note taped to the table introduces him as George, an 86-year-old farmer who died of esophageal cancer three months ago. That's all we know about him: what might pass for small talk at a newcomer's mixer in the hereafter. "And what did you do when you were alive, George?"

Besides me—and, of course, George—at the table are Stan, Hannah, Jan, Kathy, and Madeline. I've met everyone by now, except for Kathy and Madeline. Kathy is a short, attractive blond woman from the Chicago area. Madeline is in her late twenties and has long, red hair. She's actually a year ahead of us and only needs to repeat the first half of anatomy. Then she can rejoin her own class, which recently left campus for the start of their fifteen months of clinical rotations. The rest of us feel lucky to have an experienced hand on our team.

Mr. B demonstrates how to uncover our cadavers. He removes the white cotton sheet, exposing first a plastic sheet, and then a blue sheet saturated in a weak solution of pink embalming fluid. We'll be dissecting our cadavers following a time-honored sequence. The bodies will stay in the prone position for the first several days, giving us the chance to work without having to stare into George's eyes from day one.

Our dissection book explains the mechanics of what we'll be doing. We'll start by studying the many layers of back muscles, as well as vertebrae, ribs, nerves, and blood vessels. First, though, we've got to get past the process of removing some skin. We follow the book's instructions about how to hold a scalpel. The text admonishes us to just "rest your hand comfortably on the body." OK, now we look professional, maybe, but no one knows exactly how we're supposed to make the first cut. Clearly it's time for some veteran leadership, which Team George is especially fortunate to have.

"Madeline, how do we get started?" someone asks.

"I don't know," she replies in a disinterested tone, shrugging her shoulders. "Just cut."

A year removed from making her own first cut, Madeline doesn't seem all that interested in helping us neophytes along. I suspect she just wants to get out of here, rejoin her own class, and start her life. The rest of us are beginning to doubt that her guidance is going be our ace in the hole this summer.

With no help coming our way and a scalpel already in my hand, I decide to break the ice. The skin looks like vinyl, is stiffer than living tissue, and appears to be about an eighth of an inch thick. Cutting the first few inches feels very strange from an emotional perspective, but, physically, it's like cutting into a leather sofa.

After I cut along the spine for a few minutes, others are ready to step in and take turns. We keep up a running conversation about what we're seeing. Occasionally someone goes over to one of the other tables and reports back. This reconnaissance gives us hints about technique, along with opportunities to see small anatomical features that our group has already inexpertly hacked through by mistake. May Kay circulates around the room, periodically stopping at our table to uncover a new feature, such as a small nerve.

The morning goes by quickly, and soon it's time for lunch. In spite of what we've been doing, we're hungry. We retrieve our lunches from the classroom refrigerator and meet at round, cement picnic tables in an adjacent courtyard. Hands have been washed and rewashed, but we still smell the preservatives on our clothing and hair.

It's a pleasant summer day, and the breeze feels especially good after a morning of inhaling preservatives. Members of the various dissection teams are getting to know each other better, and we're also meeting people on the other teams from our occasional forays to observe their handiwork. The conversation over lunch is free and easy. One group gets teased because its cadaver has a particularly strong odor that I'm guessing they'll get used to by the end of the summer.

Our professional, yet friendly, conversations continue after lunch as we work to remove the rest of the skin and then layer upon layer of muscles until the spine and ribs are exposed. While we no longer seem to have emotional concerns with today's dissection, we do reflect on George as a person and wonder what his life was like. We're grateful that he donated his body to help us, but, even after dissecting for just a day, we're not so sure that we would want a loved one of our own to donate theirs.

After class, I walk home in the sunshine, wearing my lab outfit for fear of polluting my street clothes with the preservatives still clinging to my skin. I'm tired and sore after spending the better part of the day bent over at the waist. It's a relief to have this first day behind me. No one fainted or threw up—two of the more irrational worries some of us may have had when the day began.

Once home, I seal my anatomy gear in the garbage bag, place it in my otherwise empty dining room pantry, and take a long, hot shower. Stan stops by later to see my place for the first time. Over a beer, he talks about his life in Colorado and his old job in an adolescent psychiatric facility. He has many great stories to tell, as well as an excellent sense of humor to tell them with. He recounts some of his adventures trying to chase down escaping teenaged mental patients.

After Stan leaves, I have dinner and take a walk around my neighborhood, talking with Linda on my cell phone as I go. Actually, it's a virtual walk together, as she's walking 120 miles away with our dog. Her doctor had ordered a biopsy for some unexplained bleeding, and she received the results today. She's been told just to wait a few months and see what happens. After only a day of classes, I'm far too new a PA student to know in any detail what this might mean, but it sounds worrisome.

I pass the Women's Home, an extended-care facility where elderly residents wave back at me from their porch. A few blocks beyond is a park called the Quadranaou. A historical marker notes that the raised area in the middle of the park is an ancient, Indian holy site. A street vendor and her young son sell produce from lawn chairs in front of the park. We have a friendly conversation, and I buy some fresh sweet corn to add to my frozen meals.

Tuesdays and Thursdays are designed as catch-up days. I get to sleep in through an early morning drizzle and then walk to campus for our first radiology lecture. We learn than an X-ray image is less a picture than it is a superimposed image of all the structures that the radiation has passed through. Some structures absorb more radiation than others, making hair-line fractures, for example, dicey to find. Some of the features on an X-ray don't seem all that obvious to me.

Next, we face the college's bureaucracy to get our student ID cards. Will cashiers think mine is just a scam by some old guy to get cheap movie tickets? A perverse reversal of the scheme some underage students use to buy alcohol? In any event, technical problems intervene, and IDs can't be printed today.

I take the unexpected downtime as an opportunity to meet some more classmates. Drew is a tall, thin, outgoing guy from Florida. He lived in Columbus and worked as a tech on the trauma floor at a local hospital while waiting to get into this program. His fiancée also lives in Columbus, which is how he ended up here. He had one of the more interesting summer jobs in college: playing the tuba in a roving band at Disney World.

With a few hours of free time ahead of me, I return to the apartment for lunch and to study. After only a day, I'm already concerned about grasping all of the new concepts in anatomy. I don't think working with a cadaver is going to be as much of a problem as memorizing its myriad of features. Muscles are already an issue for me. There are hundreds of them, some spanning large segments of the body and attaching at multiple points, causing complex motions, not to mention being controlled by specific groups of nerves that we also need to memorize. We've already been given quite a bit to remember, and there is a lot of summer left to go.

Rote memorization has never been my strong suit. Fortunately, the director of the college's learning center stops by in the afternoon to help us find our own best learning styles. One of her suggestions is especially interesting: I should experiment to see which learning technique works best in each of the courses yet to come.

We're also given a calling tree so we can notify each other of schedule changes and such. These days, we're used to calling or texting anyone any time we'd like, but that wasn't the case the last time I was on a campus. My dorm had one phone for our floor and a long line of guys waiting to use it. It really didn't matter; whichever girl's dorm phone you were trying to call was probably busy anyway.

Most of my new classmates have only mobile phones, and from many different area codes. I'm one of the few here with a mobile phone and a landline. I had thought about skipping the landline, especially since we're trying to watch our expenses this year. My reason for keeping one is probably not the answer you'd expect from the riverboat gambler who quit his well-paying job to go back to school: safety. I don't expect to need emergency help, but, hey, I'm pushing sixty and live alone in a large, mostly deserted building. I'm not sure how quickly I'd be found if I called 9-1-1 on my cell.

The day ends with a mind-clearing walk through flickering clouds of lightning bugs, past the Quadranaou and surrounding neighborhoods. On nights like this, Marietta reminds me of the small New York town where I grew up. If only they put up a bed-sheet screen at the Quadranaou on Saturday nights and showed westerns. I often reflect on things while I walk, and, tonight, I reflect on a life that seems to be going well. I'm adjusting.

The next morning starts with a lecture on spinal nerves, and then we're back in the anatomy lab. Our now slightly less-clean white coats mark us as something other than total rookies. Rookie firefighters relish getting soot on their new bunker gear, and I wonder if a dirty lab coat will be a badge of pride here. Back around the metal table, we pick up where we left off. Now everyone puts in their time dissecting, and the running conversation around the table is a mix of work and friendly banter.

Lunch outside at the concrete picnic tables is also more relaxed. While there are few other students on campus at this time of year, I imagine those who do walk by can smell the preservatives on our clothing.

"We had anatomy at Ohio University last summer," Madeline recounts. "When we took our breaks in their library, some of the other students there complained about our smell. We told them, 'Hey! This is a medical school! Get over it!'"

Wedding plans seem to be a big topic of discussion. Only three of us are married, but apparently several of the others will be in the near future. RaeAnn, an outgoing woman from North Dakota, will be getting married just before we start our clinical year. Melissa is a small, quiet woman with an engaging smile and an eternally pleasant disposition. She's engaged to a pharmacy student at West Virginia University, and they plan to get married right after we graduate.

Callie, a dark-haired young woman from the Wheeling area, is engaged to a newly graduated teacher who lives in South Carolina. She hopes to do some of her clinical rotations there and get married when school ends. Kathy, a fellow member of Team George, has what sounds like a tumultuous relationship with a software engineer in Chicago. She expects to get engaged shortly, and heaven help her boyfriend if he doesn't follow through—and with the right ring—in short order.

It's only our second day of anatomy, but we're already preparing for our first exam. Anatomy tests will be a mix of written and practical exams, and, after lunch, we have a practice practical. We pick up clipboards and form up in a line snaking from station to station around the room. When a tone sounds, we move to the next station, where we find a bone, X-ray, or cadaver with a numbered pin attached to a specific feature. Before the tone sounds again, we each try to answer a question about the feature in front of us, such as, "What is this?" or "What nerve enervates this structure?"

Unfortunately, no two cadavers look exactly the same. I probably should have realized that since none of us look the same on the outside either. We get a chance to clear things up a bit in the evening when our team comes back to meet with Mark, a PA student two classes ahead of us. He's back on campus for the next few weeks, preparing to take his boards while serving as Mary Kay's lab assistant. He tries to answer our questions, but I leave the session even more confused. Somehow, I'm strangely OK with that.

Back at the apartment, there's an e-mail waiting for me from Fred, my old medic school buddy. Recently, I jokingly accused him of getting me into this PA school mess in the first place. Now he tells me that, from the tone of my messages, I must be adjusting well to my new world and that I'm prob-ably "a mature, calming, reasoned influence on the youngsters."

I'm not sure anyone has strung the words "mature," "calming," and "reasoned" together lately to describe me. In any event, his message makes me realize just how much I've already mentally integrated myself into the class. I don't feel that I'm being treated any differently than anyone else, and I like it that way. And I haven't felt the need to be an influence on anyone.

Thursday dawns cool and clear, with our school day limited to a radiol-ogy lecture and watching some infection-control films. The unstructured afternoon gives me a chance to make some more progress with my anatomy studies. I like being able to concentrate on the material without interrup-tion. In some ways, it reminds me of when I worked out of our house as a consultant. I would often get up early and start work in my pajamas, using breakfast and dressing as mid-morning breaks.

After dinner, I walk back to campus in the yellow tones of a pleasant summer evening for our first case team meeting. I'm on one of four groups that will diagnose and treat a succession of imaginary patients. In keeping with our current focus in anatomy, our first case relates to the spine and back.

We're given only basic information about our patient and his complaints. We can go on to order tests from a designated faculty member and obtain the results. At some point, we'll present our case to the rest of the class. Of course, we don't know very much about medicine after less than a week of school. Still, working together on a case is considerably more interesting than trying to remember isolated facts about, say, the oblique posterior inferior muscle.

On my way out after the meeting, I stop by Miranda's office. She's one of our instructors and I find her standing in front of a white board, busily planning clinical rotations for the class ahead of us. "Has school been much of an adjustment for you so far?" she asks.

I have to stop and think. I started here with just my small base camp, and I've been branching out ever since. I'm getting used to living alone and being in school again. "It has," I answer. "But I've decided to give myself some space and just see what happens."

She smiles. "I can understand that. Good luck."

We move from the back to the upper limbs and shoulders on Friday. Team George is getting more organized, and some division of labor is starting to take place. One student uses a copy of *Grant's Dissector* and calls out directions like a navigator in a road race, alerting the rest of the team to the next feature we're looking for. Other team members dissect or probe areas that already have been dissected.

I have to smile when I think about how I would be spending the day if I hadn't quit my job. I might be meeting with a client or working on a plan for his new project in my home office. Somehow, being here feels right, even if my academic toehold in anatomy is tenuous.

As we dissect, we're also learning more about the various personalities arrayed around George. Stan has already become my closest friend in class, and I especially appreciate his irreverent outlook. He almost always keeps his cool, regardless of how much pressure he's under.

Kathy went to Tulane in the party town of New Orleans, but eventually she graduated from a strict Christian college in Michigan. She met her fiancé Phil while making money for school as a waitress at Hooters.

Whenever she talks about Phil, it usually sounds like whatever he just did doesn't quite measure up to her exacting standards. Behind her occasionally demanding facade, I sense a good heart.

Hannah is driven, works hard, and usually has a good sense of humor, but she can be quick to anger. She and Kathy really don't seem all that far apart in temperament, but they sometimes don't see eye to eye. When that happens, Stan just takes a break and walks away from the drama. Kind of like my friendly dog quietly moving away from boisterous children.

Jan grew up not far from here. She's down to earth, like many of the locals I've met so far. She is the first person in her family to go to college, and, in spite of already having a master's degree, she seems to feel that she's at something of a disadvantage academically. She asks a lot of questions in class and takes some not always gentle kidding about it.

Madeline just seems anxious to get out of town, which probably explains why she doesn't try very hard to bond with the rest of us. It seems every day she languishes here is just another day she has fallen behind her classmates in their clinical rotations.

It's late in the day when I leave the personalities of Team George behind and drive three hours to my part-time job as a paramedic in London, Ohio. I used to do this almost every Friday night, partially for the experience, partially to spend time with what has become my second family, and partially to preserve that thread of purpose I started following all those years ago as a hospital volunteer. Strictly speaking, PA students are not supposed to have jobs. Early on, I told the program office that I just wanted to maintain my patient-care skills. They have agreed to let me work two nights a month, as long as it doesn't interfere with school.

Soon I'm back among old friends at Madison County EMS Station 281. Tonight I'm with the 1 Unit crew, one of three groups of EMTs and paramedics staffing the station around the clock, twenty-four hours on and forty-eight off. London is the seat of a mostly rural county bisected by Interstate 70, just west of Columbus. There'll be no studying here tonight. Instead, between runs, I catch up on my crewmates' lives and tell them about my early adventures at college.

Unvarnished conversation is a big part of station life. It often involves humor and, sometimes, crude stories, but also heartfelt discussions about family problems and personal aspirations. We count on each other in the street, and a crew has the feel of a family, even for part-timers like me. The 1 Unit crew of Medic 282 works, talks, laughs, eats, and naps its way through another night of emergency calls.

One of our runs on this muggy summer night takes place just after two in the morning, which, under the best of conditions, is a disorienting time for me. Since now I could be sleeping in any of three cities, when the PA system comes on to dispatch our run, it takes me an extra second or two to remember where I am.

We've been called to a local all-night convenience store, where we find a disheveled twenty-six-year-old man sitting on the ground. Flashing red and blue lights from the responding police cars illuminate his face, and we can see blood oozing from a wound near his left eye. Three police officers are on the scene, so things seem under control. Our patient has the smell of beer on his breath as he tells his story.

He's not exactly sure what happened; he either was struck in the face or he struck the pavement when he fell. He didn't get a good look at his assailant, and he's understandably angry about the whole episode. We check him out with our flashlights. Aside from the deep laceration on his face, he has a minor abrasion on his hip. Our procedure for injuries of this type is to place the patient on a backboard as a precaution, but he'll have none of that. After considerable encouragement, he finally agrees to let us bandage his wound and take him to the hospital, where they'll suture the laceration and rule out a closed head injury. Then, after readying the truck for another run and doing the paperwork, it's back to bed for us.

I'm up early Saturday morning, with the first order of business being to make sure that my day-shift replacement has arrived. I spot him; there's a new lump sleeping under a blanket in one of the lounge's easy chairs. I collect my gear and quietly slip out of the building.

An hour later, I'm sitting in a diner near our home, wearing the same rumpled uniform I've slept in and nursing a welcome cup of hot coffee. Soon, Linda comes in, a big smile on her face, and I stand to give her a hug. I wonder if the other customers think we're lovers meeting secretly, though I'm hardly dressed for it, and Gail's Diner isn't much of a romantic getaway. It's great to see her after another week apart, and we share news of our respective worlds. Later, we take our dog Skyler to a local park. He seems happy to see me, too.

By Sunday afternoon, it's already time to leave, and, a few hours later, I'm unloading supplies at my Marietta outpost. This rapid context switch from being home with my family one minute and then back here alone the next still isn't routine for me.

CHAPTER 5

STRIKE ONE

Marietta, Monday, June 28

We spend most of Monday under Mary Kay's smiling tutelage while we focus on the nerves and muscles of the arm. New material just keeps piling atop the only slightly less new. The first few days of anatomy were enlightening, what with new things to learn, new people to work with, and what already looks like a bottomless pit of new stories for my civilian friends back home. But with our first exam now only a week away, reality is starting to set in.

Lewis and Clark probably had moments like this. Their merry band paddles away from St. Louis, goes around a bend in the Missouri—shouts of encouragement still ringing in their ears—and suddenly they realize just how hard it's going to be, crossing a continent against the current.

Give me a series of related facts, and I can usually find a way to organize and remember them. Isolated facts are another story. Now I'm supposed to remember that the wrist bones are the lunate, scaphoid, triquetrum, pisaform, hamate, capitate, trapezoid, and trapezium? That's another kettle of Latin fish entirely.

We cut away at George's features day after day, and I'm still not grasping the facts. Sometimes the very process of dissection seems to get in the way. Following our dissection guidebook like a map results, not so surprisingly, in something very much like a road trip. We don't dwell on the nice cornfield we've just passed. Instead, we're focused on finding the next turn. And we can't go back for another look; our scalpels are like bulldozers, obliterating the cornfields as we pass.

It's said that Albert Einstein defined insanity as doing the same thing over and over and expecting a different result. Albert and I finally decide that it's time to find another way to study. After all, the learning center director did say that we should experiment with learning styles. I order flash cards with the muscles highlighted and pay a premium so that they'll get here by tomorrow. I just hope that's soon enough.

I walk to campus after dinner, where I pick up a box of synthetic bones and sit on the classroom floor, my anatomy book open by my side. It feels a lot like putting a kid's bike together on Christmas Eve. Except, this time, the instructions aren't in English. Come to think of it, most assembly instructions do seem like they're written in another language. Jan stops by after a while, and we start working together. She was an athletic trainer as an undergrad and certainly knows her bones and muscles.

Back at the apartment, I find an e-mail with an electronic copy of our class picture. Let's see...who looks out of place? Oh, yes, there I am. I send a copy to Fred, my retired dentist friend. He's out there, somewhere in the ether, now safely past the rapids of anatomy and soon to reach the high plains of his clinical rotations.

His response: "Don't let those youngsters get to you. We have experience on our side." Yes, Fred, and probably several million fewer functioning neurons.

Being surrounded by the sea of youth in the class picture reminds me of someone I haven't thought about in years. During my undergraduate days, we had a guest in our dorm, a retired air force sergeant who had taken classes all over the world from the University of Maryland's extension program. In those days, the rule was that you had to put in at least one semester on campus in order to graduate. And that's how a fifty-year-old retired guy ended up living in Cambridge A Hall with a bunch of us youngsters.

His wife and kids were waiting for him in Sundance, Wyoming, which is why we started out calling him The Sundance Kid. Ultimately, though, it was Sarge that stuck. I'm sure that he wanted to be out of college and back with his family then at least as much as Madeline does now.

Most nights would find Sarge studying in his room, wearing his trademark rimless glasses. It was rare that someone wasn't sitting on his bed, chattering away, while Sarge sat at his desk and tried vainly to study. Always the gentleman, he'd stop and talk about whatever his young visitor might want to discuss. More often than not, it was that great mystery of our young lives: women. Sarge would usually just laugh and impart some thoughtful bit of information. Not always useful to us, at least then, but thoughtful nonetheless.

We enjoyed having Sarge around. Even though he was our fathers' age, the lack of a lifelong relationship with him seemed to bridge the years between us more smoothly. Sarge would be in his late eighties by now, and I hope he's doing well tonight, wherever he may be.

Wednesday brings another full day of anatomy, along with one of those strange connections we sometimes come across in life. When I took organic chemistry seven years ago, Yadwiga was the professional chemist in my class who helped me survive during my first months back in a chemistry lab. Today I learn that one of my new classmates, Joanna, is actually Yadwiga's daughter. Her mom recognized me from our class picture.

Organic chemistry was the first prerequisite I took, so I was then just at the beginning of what turned out to be a long road to PA school. And now, here I am. Joanna laughs when I tell her that I hope to graduate before yet another generation of her family gets a chance to witness my academic journey.

Tonight it's time to branch out a little for dinner, so I decide to make fish. To be honest, that just means spraying oil on my one oven dish, adding two pieces of frozen fish, and baking the assembly for thirty minutes. I add some corn from the neighborhood produce stand and wash it all down with a beer while watching the news. Total luxury.

Other than a quick trip to school for a radiology lecture, I spend most of Thursday parading around my apartment, reciting the names of bones, muscles, and nerves, along with their functions. Our dissection team meets after dinner for a review, but we really don't know what to expect from next week's test. Except, perhaps, for Madeline, and she continues to pass along very little in the way of useful information.

Madeline is not the only one thinking about life after anatomy. Kathy and RaeAnn ask if they can spend the night at our house when the term ends and then catch flights home the following morning. I'm sure that will be fine, and I let Linda know by e-mail. She responds—copying the rest of the family—that, after being a college student for only a few weeks, "he's already inviting women to spend the night."

We spend most of Friday in the lab, reviewing the back and upper limb for Monday's test. After class, Stan, Drew, and I celebrate the start of the weekend, joking as we walk up the Fourth Street hill, invisible trails of formaldehyde stretching out behind us. Drew is in another dissection group and has become a good friend of Stan's. A perennially cheerful guy, he lives just a block away from me.

Drew and Stan peel off at their respective intersections, and I continue on to find Linda and Skyler waiting for me. They're staying overnight, on their way to visit Linda's mother in Maryland. It's good to see them both.

Linda and I want to walk around town, but first Skyler has to find a spot to relieve himself. He has never been away from home before and wanders aimlessly behind the apartment, looking for something familiar. Eventually I lead him to a spot that looks a little bit like our backyard at home. Don't sweat it, Skyler; it's taken me a while to find my place here, too.

Linda leaves Saturday morning, and I spend most of the day studying. I'm browsing the web after dinner when I come across what surely is a fake contest to win a billion dollars. The ad lists some of the things that you could do with the money. I'm somewhat surprised to realize that, if I won, I wouldn't change what I'm doing right now. Not that our family's standard of living wouldn't change! With that reassuring thought, I settle into Al's old easy chair and watch *The Legend of Bagger Vance*.

Sunday morning, the Fourth of July, is sunny and warm. I decide to start the holiday with a big breakfast at the Shoney's on the edge of town. This time of year, many of my fellow diners are probably tourists pausing on their way to or from the Carolina beaches, where Ohioans migrate with a regularity rivaling salmon runs on the Columbia River. But I'm a local now and have no inclination to rush back onto to the Interstate. I splurge on a Sunday paper, accompanied by a breakfast of sausage, eggs, and a bottomless cup of decaf.

I spend the rest of the day studying, the summer heat periodically relieved by thunderstorms rumbling through town. Rain drums on the sidewalk outside my open window while I sit in Al's chair and review my notes. Linda and Skyler stop by later, on their way back from Maryland, and spend the night. Skyler sleeps just outside our bedroom door, and, for the night anyway, we're a pack again.

Marietta, Monday, July 5

This hot, steamy day is anything but a national holiday for the twenty-one of us about to face our first anatomy exam. We've studied for weeks, using all the techniques we can think of. We've probed the cadavers. We've studied pictures. We've taken practice exams. I've paraded around my apartment, reciting the names of bones, muscles, and nerves. Kathy had her fiancé ask her questions over the phone for hours, but, unfortunately, he ended up getting chastised for somehow "doing it wrong."

Preparations behind us now, we gather in the computer room for the written part of the exam. It turns out to be difficult, but I don't think I could have done any better if there had been another six months to study. After clicking the submit button, I cross the hall to the clinical room and sprawl out on one of its padded benches to rest.

Gaggles of students drift in, engaged in animated conversations about specific questions. I want to plug my ears; the more possible answers I hear, the more questions I'm convinced I've gotten wrong. Fortunately we soon learn that no one received less than a C. That just leaves the daunting practical exam after lunch.

We find our cadavers arranged around the lab, along with X-rays, plastic bones, and computer displays. Pins and questions have been strategically placed, and, clipboards in hand, we silently serpentine around the room each time the buzzer sounds. When we complete the circuit, Mary Kay collects our answer sheets and begins announcing the correct choices.

Early on, I get a sinking feeling that I've missed a great many questions. As Mary Kay works through her list, there is a rustling in our midst, and a woman dashes out of the room in tears. I find her later in the clinical room, her eyes still red from crying. She reminds me of my daughter after one of her tougher college exams. And, for the moment, I feel more like a father than a student who just blew the same test. I tell her that I'm sure she did well enough and that we'll all get better with time. She smiles weakly.

Student once more, I leave to catch up with classmates on their way for a well-deserved post-exam beer. We cross the Muskingum River on a rusting railway bridge that has been converted into a pedestrian walkway and then traverse the final block to the Harmar Tavern. I've been beating myself up the whole way, and my classmates don't seem any happier. The Harmar is a good place to be right now, and our mood slowly improves as talk of the test dwindles away.

Later I send an e-mail description of the day to my family. Katie answers, describing her first anatomy test in veterinary school eight years ago:

> I did terribly. I thought, 'Oh, no. This is going to be a long 4 years!' Luckily, it got easier from there once I knew what to expect. Also, identifying organs is much easier than muscles, especially spinal muscles (which all look exactly the same and usually have almost the same names).

I appreciate the encouragement from the people I love. That seems to be the case for some of the others, too. Jan's e-mail tonight has a new signature block:

Jan —, ATC/L, NREMT-B, ACI
Marietta College Physician Assistant Program Student
Wife of Jonathan, the best husband ever!

It's raining Tuesday, a fitting backdrop for the unveiling of our newly posted grades. I did well enough on the written exam, but I was one of the bottom two or three on the practical. Because the two grades average, I pass, but far below the class average. I eventually send Gloria an e-mail, more or less apologizing for my performance, and her answer is encouraging. Overall, she feels our class did a good job, because usually there are "more students in trouble" at this point. It's just uncomfortable being one of them.

Running errands during a gap in the schedule, I find a pair of Linda's socks in my wash at the Laundromat. I have to laugh; I'm supposed to be bringing my laundry home, not the other way around.

CHAPTER 6

FRIENDS

Marietta, Wednesday, July 7

I t's time to roll our cadavers onto their backs. We've glanced at George's face from time to time, but, up to now, only in profile. The head-on view is somewhat disconcerting at first. After spending a few moments quietly looking, we gently cover his face with a towel moistened in preservative. It will stay that way until near the end of the term, when we study the head. We spend the rest of the day opening the chest and studying its structures.

Mary Kay motions me aside as class ends. "I was wondering," she asks. "Why did you do so well on the written test and...not as well...on the practical?"

Very diplomatically put, I think. I try to describe my problems with memorization and relating features to nearby landmarks. Mary Kay tells me that our class is doing well and that I shouldn't be too concerned at this point. One of my reasons for coming here seems to be validated: the faculty does seem to care how I'm doing.

We have tomorrow off to make up for having had our exam on a national holiday, so there is a class party tonight. After a shower to wash away the lab smell and with some beer and chips to share, I walk to a classmate's house.

Natalie greets me at the door. A striking young woman with large, dark eyes and black hair, she went to Marietta as an undergraduate and still lives with some of the same roommates. I join my classmates in the backyard, where I meet Melanie. She started out in the class just ahead of us, with Madeline, but she will be joining us this fall. Until then, she's working in a downtown art gallery.

Most of the evening's conversation is about school, and I fit in just fine. Then two of the guests start talking about how they want to skip their upcoming fifth and tenth high school reunions, respectively. Ouch. My high school class is having its fortieth in a few weeks, and I'm probably the only one missing it because he's still in school.

By ten o'clock, most of the group decides that it's time to leave for The Double L, a bar downtown. After that, in RaeAnn's words, "We will see where the night leads us." For someone forty years out of high school, it leads to bed, so I wish them well.

I celebrate a warm, sunny day off by sleeping in until seven o'clock. It takes all of twenty minutes for my weekly cleaning blitz through the apartment, and then I study until Stan calls to suggest lunch at the Third Street Deli. He has moved out of the dorm and now lives on the first floor of a rental house. Our classmate Joanna lives upstairs.

We walk to campus later for a class picnic. Gloria is there, socializing and taking pictures. She seems pleased that a group of twenty-one students who didn't know each other just a few weeks ago has started to bond. We also meet up with Drew, his fiancée, Jodi, and his parents. Having visited family in Michigan, Jack and Karen are passing through town to see their son. Jack is a minister and a few years younger than me. As they're about to leave for the return trip to Florida, he takes me aside.

"I really envy your chance to go back to school," he says with a smile. "Good luck!"

An impromptu kickball game breaks out under the trees next to our classroom building. In spite of being a few steps slower than my teammates, I have a good time. Drew describes the game later in an e-mail to the class:

> For all who did not attend on Thursday for kickball, you missed a great game! I believe the final score was 63-64:) (Jeff's call)

> To recap some of the game's highlights: we had Joanna sliding ON home plate for a good 5 feet before the cardboard came to rest. Kevin, I didn't know the man could move so quickly! A great slide to second by Seren. Kim, Barry, Aaron, Jeff, and Seren, to name a few, were playing the outfield making great plays and chasing all the foul balls! And I can't forget to

mention the tree that got in the game numerous times and seemed to help out both sides!

Thanks to Kim for supplying the grill, and thanks to everyone for bringing food. I think the next step is starting a MC Kickball team and going to the state level. Just kidding. Peace ya'll!

We troop back to lab the next morning. It's a warm, sunny Friday, and we're refreshed from our day off. We're focusing on the heart and surrounding blood vessels today. George had a strong, healthy heart, unlike some of the other cadavers in the room.

I've never before given much thought as to how our organs develop in the womb. We learn that the heart starts development near the throat and slowly migrates into the chest. A nerve controlling part of the larynx is caught up in the aortic arch and has to lengthen as the heart descends. Ultimately, this "recurrent laryngeal nerve" takes a long detour from the neck into the chest and back again, putting it at risk for accidental damage during surgery.

When classes end for the week, I load two weeks' worth of dirty laundry and recycling into the car and drive home. A few hours later, I'm back in Westerville, sitting on our deck with Linda, sipping wine and grilling dinner. Life is good. While lightning bugs wink in our yard, I try to sum up the past few weeks. Sure, I've been bloodied on my first big exam, but I'm not discouraged. Sometimes I feel like one of the gang, and sometimes I feel old. Overall, though, I've made friends, and I'm comfortable with my new situation.

Weekends are busy times for home owners, especially for those like me who are gone all week and have stacks of mail to go through and bills to pay. We also try to keep up with family and friends, which helps me stay grounded as a middle-aged adult between my weekly forays into college life. This morning, for example, I have one of my regular monthly breakfasts with Bill. I treasure our friendship and his excellent sense of humor. Today's stories about the frustrations of corporate life reaffirm my decision to have gotten out of that environment twelve years ago.

Our family comes over for brunch on Sunday. Tom and Katie's lives are all about preparations for their first child this fall. Gary is living in a condo with Daniel, who is working full-time as a newspaper reporter and part-time at a local radio station.

Although I look forward to the upcoming week at school, being with my family for even a few hours reminds me of all that I am missing out on this year. On my drive back to Marietta, I listen to Daniel on the radio until his voice fades into the static a few miles short of my apartment.

Marietta, Monday, July 12

There is a new sign posted on our classroom refrigerator, a takeoff on a familiar Visa ad:

- Soda: 50 cents.
- Muffins: 50 cents.
- Smelling like a cadaver all summer: priceless.

Team George spends another day on the chest, getting familiar with what is where. After class, Stan and I visit the Harmar Tavern. More a local joint than a typical college bar, it is fast becoming one of the class's favorite haunts. Its smoky main room has beer-advertising paraphernalia on its knotty pine walls, along with the hood of a race car. A leather wall hanging lists the names and dates of the bar's various owners since 1900.

Over a dinner of the Harmar's self-proclaimed soon-to-be-famous fried-bologna sandwiches and beer, Stan tells me more about his life's highlights thus far. He's had an interesting time of it, having run with the bulls in Pamplona and studied in a Buddhist monastery in China. It's clear he likes adventure, and that won't end with PA school. He talks about becoming a police officer someday, or perhaps joining the army. His sense of humor, love of adventure, energy, and relaxed nature make him a joy to be around.

I found a promising anatomy study tool last weekend while poking around the Internet. It's ADAM, a computer program that lets you navigate cleanly through the layers of the body and isolate features. In other words, the way our dissection team would with George if we were better at dissection than we actually are. ADAM seems worth a try, so I've ordered it. Penny, our program's administrative assistant, ducks into our classroom Tuesday to announce its arrival.

I take ADAM back to the apartment and spend the rest of the day experimenting with it, along with reading 150 pages of abdominal anatomy before tomorrow's lab. After dinner, I meet Stan, Seren, and Drew downtown for a few games of pool. When we finish, the lads start an improbable search for donuts. That is, until Seren spots bigger game: some young women sitting together in a nearby bar. The single guys decide to forgo the great donut hunt and go in. I wish them luck and head for home, feeling a little like Sarge probably did back in the day.

It's noticeably cooler Wednesday as we gather for Mary Kay's introduction to the abdomen. We're given a long list of structures to find in lab today, and, for some reason, our team is missing more of them than usual. Hopefully ADAM will let me find structures on my computer that we've accidentally hacked through in real life.

We spend Thursday learning about abdominal X-rays and parceling out our case team's work for our next imaginary patient. We return to lab on Friday for another full day of dissection, and I'm beat by the time I straggle back to the apartment. I'm spending virtually all of my waking, nonclass time using ADAM, and I think it's starting to help.

With another exam coming up early next week, I've decided to stay in town this weekend to study. I get started early Saturday, taking a break in the late afternoon when Linda and Skyler drop by for a visit. Skyler happily rediscovers his patch of ground, and, later, Linda and I have dinner with my neighbor Bruce and his wife.

Sunday morning starts with coffee on my front stoop, followed by a walk to the Lafayette Hotel for breakfast. The old hotel sits at the confluence of the Muskingum and Ohio Rivers, where Lafayette came ashore to visit in the early 1800s. We wander along the river after breakfast, past a park dedicated by FDR in the 1930s to commemorate the founding of the Northwest Territory. Soon Linda and Skyler are on the road, and I'm taking another practice exam in the lab.

Marietta, Monday, July 19

The week begins in full test-preparation mode. If I'm awake, I'm either in class, in the lab, or studying at the apartment. When the clock radio goes off Tuesday, it wakes me with a story about today being the thirty-fifth anniversary of the *Apollo 11* moon landing. The announcer's tone suggests that this event is ancient history, something like the signing of the *Magna Carta*, I suppose.

I wasn't at Runnymede in 1215, but the twenty-three-year-old version of me was at Cape Canaveral for the launch of *Apollo 11*, along with Mom, Linda, and my brother. Dad worked in Launch Control while the rest of us watched the liftoff from just a few miles away. I can still remember the tremendous roar of the engines, the huge flocks of startled birds, and my shirt buttons rattling against my chest.

Back on earth thirty-five years later, it's test day, and my study techniques seem to work well enough on the written portion. The challenging practical exam is coming up after I have lunch with Stan and Drew at Brownie's Market.

Brownie's is in an old building on Front Street, where the black-and-white–checkered floor has been well worn by generations of Marietta students and townies alike. It's the place to go for pepperoni rolls, which are sticks of pepperoni wrapped in dough and sold two to an unmarked baggie.

You can warm your purchase to suit your taste in a small microwave oven on the counter.

Soon enough, the pleasant taste of lunchtime pepperoni is just a memory as we pick up clipboards, pencils, and answer sheets and silently move around the room. We're snaking past cadavers that, by now, have been heavily—though not expertly—dissected. Not to be indelicate, but today's chore is something like looking for specific meat fibers in a pot roast. When we finish, Mary Kay reads through the correct choices, and I think maybe I've done better this time. Any progress would be appreciated.

But some things don't change. Again I find a classmate crying in the clinical room, but not the same young woman this time. "I *hate* anatomy," she declares fiercely through her tears. "And I've *always* hated it."

I've got my own feelings about anatomy these days, but I think I'll keep them to myself. "It just was a hard test," I say softly. "I'm sure you'll do better next time."

"No! You don't understand!" she sputters. "I really *have* always hated anatomy. Even the essay in my school application was about how much I hate it!"

I can understand her frustrations, but her words make me smile. I remember being young enough to think that writing something negative on an application was somehow a good idea. And, over the years, I've heard similar statements from my own kids. I try to be supportive and invite her to join us for our now-traditional post-exam beer. She shows up later, tears long forgotten.

Later, Stan stops by my apartment at the end of his nightly run. Like several others in our class, he runs for exercise, often at odd hours. As the only self-described "running Asian" in a very Caucasian town, he feels a little out of place, but he's getting used to it.

By Stan's calculation, today is a milestone: we're halfway through the summer semester and 10 percent through our so-called didactic year on campus. He also passes on some news he picked up on campus. Team George is down to four students; Madeline passed today's exam and, at last, is on her way to a long-delayed family practice rotation. Our tardy student ID cards have also arrived, so now I have the option of buying cheap movie tickets at either end of the age continuum: student ID or AARP card.

Thursday morning's walk to school is past the now-familiar classic homes with wide front porches and flower gardens. Once in our classroom area, I find a gaggle of students standing in front of a bulletin board. They're looking for their exam grades, and I join them, searching for the last four digits of my social security number. Ah, there it is. I did fine on the written test and about average on the practical, which is a substantial improvement. At this point, that's more than good enough for me.

After a short medical terminology quiz, we're free for the rest of the day. I decide to cross the Ohio River and explore the West Virginia side. My big discovery there, just across the bridge from Marietta, is an ATM for my bank in Columbus. It's the only one I've found anywhere in the area.

While Lewis and Clark would laugh at my minor inconveniences, finding the ATM is a big deal for me. After all, I'm really just camping out in Marietta. I go home most weekends with an empty wallet and a full load of recycling and dirty clothes. When I come back on Sunday, it's with cash, frozen food, bottled water, and clean laundry. Now, in addition to local fall-backs for food, water, and laundry, I've got one for cash.

It's just a lot tamer on the Ohio now than it was in your day, Captain Lewis.

CHAPTER 7
SHAKEN DREAMS

Marietta, Friday, July 23

A rainstorm passed through town overnight, and this morning is sunny, cool, and clear. It's a pleasant walk to campus at the start of what looks like a beautiful summer day. Adding to my general feeling of contentment is the thought that, after six weeks of trying everything I can think of, I may finally have brought anatomy under control.

Or maybe not. Instead of Mary Kay, we find a new lecturer for our next unit. Dr. S is a fit-looking man of about fifty. Some of the women in class already have learned that he was once "Mr. Ohio" in a category of bodybuilding. While he is fit and knowledgeable, he quickly proves to be terminally disorganized.

Dr. S presents, almost randomly, from a disorganized pile of transparencies. Each overhead is a diagram with unlabeled lines pointing to various anatomical features. He jumps from slide to slide, rapidly introducing new features. We frantically search through our handouts, trying to find the one he's lecturing from so we can take notes. By the time we've found the right page, he has zoomed off in yet another direction. After ten minutes of this, I'm hopelessly lost.

Fortunately, we're dissecting the sex organs today, so, notes or not, at least I know where to look. No one on our team is in a hurry to remove George's suddenly very public privates, but, eventually, we do, with great respect and care. A few minutes later, Dr. S joins us and begins pointing out features. Before we know it, he has picked up a scalpel and quickly cuts the penis crosswise, like a hot dog. This sends a shiver up my spine, and Stan,

53

the only other male in our group, gives me a sickly look. Maybe we're not as hardened to all this as we thought.

Linda is in town for tonight's class party. Our hosts are Aaron and his wife, Liz, who have a two-story townhouse on the Ohio River. As we pull up, a game of cornhole is under way in the front yard. Most of the class is already here, drinks in hand, and animated conversations are under way. Linda gradually connects the people she meets with the stories I've been telling her. We stay late to meet Kathy's boyfriend, Phil, a quiet, likeable guy who has been driving all evening to get here from Chicago.

We leave Saturday morning for a quick trip to visit Linda's mother, and, by dinnertime, we're on her Maryland farm. This is the first time I've been back since school started, and an impromptu family reunion is under way. Linda's two brothers and their families are here, along with my parents, who have driven up from their home in the Washington suburbs. There is conversation and laughter over what has become a family tradition: a Chinese take-out dinner.

Just a few feet from where we're sitting tonight is the spot where I first met Ed, my late father-in-law. On a winter night almost forty years ago, Linda woke him to pull her date's car out of a snow-filled ditch with his tractor. He didn't say much that night, but he did have a big smile on his face. I last saw him three years ago, not far from the same spot, taking a short walk in the snow with our son Gary.

Before we leave, the family meets for Sunday breakfast and then drives into the Catoctin Mountains to visit Ed's grave, not far from Camp David. It's under a tree in a small cemetery next to an old country church. We plant some flowers, and then each of us leaves a small stone of remembrance atop his headstone.

Marietta, Monday, July 26

We're dissecting the digestive tract in lab today, and I reflect on how this isn't all that routine a task for the odd Monday afternoon. Then again, my days aren't so routine anymore. When we've finished our work, surprisingly it is Team George that has managed to do a near-perfect job of dissection, especially of the various muscle groups at the...er...terminal end. Now, for a change, George is the cadaver that the other groups want to learn from and, one by one, they wander over to admire our handiwork. "You show them, Barry," one of my partners suggests.

"OK. I'll be your rear admiral, today," I quip to one group. "Let me take you on a tour of the anus." This gets big laughs, but I may also have given myself an unfortunate new nickname.

Most of the time, I can't remember any of my dreams the next morning. For some reason, though, I do remember one on Tuesday. With all of the studying, I expect to have some medical themes creep in, and occasionally they do. But last night's dream is the first I can recall that starred our grandson. He's not due for another three months, but he must already be on my mind.

In the dream, he's just a few days old and staying with us while his parents are out of town. I'm cradling him and cooing like you would expect to do with a baby. Suddenly he looks me squarely in the eyes with a serious expression on his face. In spite of his tender age, he starts talking in perfect English, letting me know in no uncertain terms that he doesn't appreciate being cooed at. Apparently that is downright demeaning for a liberated baby like my grandson. He tells me that he prefers to be called by a specific name that, unfortunately, I have since forgotten. Hopefully it wasn't Chucky.

With just a week left before our next exam, and with my anxiety level rising, I decide to try to add some organization to Dr. S's lectures. Before he starts this morning, I ask if I can number his overheads with a grease pencil. He looks puzzled as to why I would want to do that, but he humors me anyway. While the rest of the class numbers their handout pages consecutively, I try to number his already out-of-order overheads. It helps a little, but he's still too fast for us.

While my hope for surviving anatomy remains in intensive care, another dream is literally biting the dust back at the apartment. Business has been slow for the wedding planners, and the two young owners are closing down their shop. Sometimes enthusiasm alone isn't enough.

I spend Thursday in my apartment with Dr. S's incomprehensible handouts and the ADAM software. Team George continues its slog through the pelvis and peritoneum on Friday, and, after class, I load the car for a weekend at home. Usually I try not to study at home, but with the troubles I've been having, I make an exception and bring my books with me.

My weekend home actually starts with an evening on the squad in London. I'm with my 3 Unit friends tonight and manage to arrive just in time for dinner with Tommy, Matt, Carolyn, and Scott. Over a traditional firehouse meal of hearty portions of meat and potatoes, we tease Tommy about the current population of his house. His three adult children—and their children—come, go, and return again. I've offered my basement to him, should he ever just want some peace and quiet.

Matt is an earnest guy in his late twenties. He was accepted to medical school a few years ago, but he and his wife decided that wasn't the lifestyle for them. They want to have a family and more time together than Matt's physician father was able to spend with him. He often talks about entering a PA or nurse practitioner program someday.

Carolyn has a ready smile and a good word for everyone. She's a determined divorced mom of two and wants very badly for her children to succeed. Scott is the newest member of the crew and the perfect foil for Matt. Both are physically big men, and they love to tease one another.

"Will we be 'spooning' again tonight?" jokes Matt. All the men sleep in single beds in the same bunk room.

"Nah," Scott replies. "Given our size, it would be more like 'ladling' anyway."

The crew gives good patient care and has a tradition of maintaining its cool, even when the situation becomes chaotic. But they can play, too. I'm on the first truck out tonight, with Matt and Scott. Matt decides we should play a game. "Tonight," he suggests, "let's use the word 'davenport' at least once in conversation with each of our patients."

On our first run, we encounter an elderly man lying on his living room floor with an apparently dislocated hip. From my standpoint, this is convenient because we've been covering hip injuries in class. From Matt's perspective, it's the perfect time to start our game.

"Sir, did you fall on your way to the davenport?" Matt asks, without cracking a smile.

"What? No!" says the patient, with an incredulous expression on his face. "I was going to the front door to get my mail!"

I awake Saturday morning from a last, precious sliver of sleep, quietly collect my gear, and meet Linda at Gail's Diner for breakfast. Later, we meet my old paramedic classmate Fred and his wife, Maureen, for dinner and a play. Fred has nearly finished his classroom year at a PA school near Cleveland, and he's getting ready for his clinical rotations. He has been consumed with school, putting in herculean hours and obsessing over every detail. "My instructors tell me that science doesn't yet know the answers to some of my questions," he laments.

While Katie and our son-in-law, Tom, are over for Sunday brunch, Linda's brother Ted calls to tell us that their Aunt Eleanor has died. She was my father-in-law's eldest sister, had exceptional manners, knew every card game ever invented, and was one of my favorite relatives to talk to at family reunions. Her children were with her when she died, a lady to the end.

I decide to take the scenic route back to Marietta, driving along the Muskingum River on State Route 60 until it reaches my front door. As usual, I listen to Daniel on the radio as I go, until he fades away for another week. The closer I get to town, the more I think about the upcoming test. I'll have to get right back to my books.

It isn't long after I get to the apartment that I realize my books are missing. They are in my book bag, which is still hanging on my office door-knob at home, 120 miles away. In spite of my best intentions, I never even opened them over the weekend, and now I need them badly. With no time to waste, a pointless four-hour trip ahead of me, and anger rising at my own stupidity, I slam the car door and start for the interstate. Somehow I have got to get them and get back here in time for a case team meeting tonight.

I get angry more often than I would like, even though it almost always makes things worse. When I finally calm down this time, I realize that there is a silver lining: if I had left the books in London, this would be a pointless six-hour trip instead. And with renewed calm comes the return of some basic problem-solving skills. I think to call Linda, who retrieves the book bag and starts driving towards me. Our paths finally cross (thanks to mobile phones), the books are exchanged, and I get back just in time for the meeting.

Marietta, Monday, August 2

We're focusing on the hip, knee, and ankle today. By the time we finish, George is in several pieces.

The next morning, I'm up before dawn in full exam-preparation mode on what looks to be the beginning of a scorching summer day. I pore through my notes and then walk back to campus to work through a box of plastic bones. I try to memorize all of the various spines, processes, fossae, foramina, tubercles, notches, and other lower extremity minutia that we're expected to know. Most of the evening is spent trying to memorize the muscles. Stan drops by to see if I can tell him what a "femoral torsion angle" is. Surprisingly, I can, in one of my few moments of clarity all day.

I'm up early again Wednesday—test day—but, in the end, it really doesn't matter. The exam probes deeply into obscure recesses of the mate-rial, and, once again, I've done poorly. After a brief flash of success on our second exam, this third one has found its way back into the loss column.

Gathering at the Harmar later with my classmates, I can see that I'm not alone in my funk. I don't say much about it to the others, but now I'm firmly entrenched in self-doubt. I've gotten past a lot in my life, but I just don't see how I can still pass anatomy with only one exam to go. Maybe next summer I'll be just an older, male version of Madeline, held over with next year's class while my friends move on with their clinical rotations. Or worse. Maybe I'm like the aging athlete who tries to play one season too many. Maybe I really am a few million neurons short of a full load.

Walking home from the Harmar, I'm wallowing in the hopelessness of it all when something new pops into my head. Suddenly I realize that I've been looking at my grades as some kind of cosmic sign. As in, "I got an A. Obviously I was right to quit my job and go back to school." At last I realize how decidedly unhelpful this perspective really is. I chose this mission: school, the twenty-seven months without an income, the tuition, the living expenses, the separation from my family, and the career all this will prepare me for. And, now that I'm on it, grades aren't cosmic signs of anything. They're just grades.

All I really want to do is stay here, regardless of my grades. *I just want to pass so I can get a chance to see what happens next.* As a practical matter, I don't know if it's still possible to pass. One thing I do know is that, if it's still statistically possible, it will mean preparing differently for our last remaining exam. I'm not sure yet what preparing differently will mean, but this is one old guy who's on a mission and up to finding out.

My neighbor Bruce stops by later for a chat. He's buying a house so he and his wife can finally live together again, and he'll be moving out of his apartment soon. Still later, I fall asleep to the noisy dismantling of a dream on the other side of my bedroom wall. By morning, all traces of the wedding planning business are gone.

CHAPTER 8

TWO-A-DAYS

Marietta, Thursday, August 5

A cool overnight breeze has chased away the summer heat, and I walk to campus enjoying the crisp morning. I find chalk scratches in front of one of the now-familiar homes announcing the upcoming arrival of a baby brother. New life is in the air, I've come to terms with my grades, and tonight I will be meeting Linda for a belated anniversary dinner. All in all, it should be a good day.

While we wait in the computer lab for the day to get under way, we study, play online games, or surf the web. Stan has found an elaborate game site. Jeff is watching what, at least to me, are really gross videos that he finds especially funny. Julia is designing custom athletic shoes on a website that lets her choose her own designs. Kathy and Jen are checking their e-mail.

After a brief medical terminology quiz, we cross over into the classroom to find a very good omen. Mary Kay is back for the skull, the last part of the body that we will be covering this summer. Today is spent in the dry lab, where we handle dried skulls and plastic models. We cover the names, locations, and functions of 104 features associated with just the bony parts of the skull. We'll learn the softer, squishier parts during our final weeks in lab with George.

Today's dry lab seems strangely familiar. Then I remember why: this is the very class Linda and I peeked in on last summer during our campus visit. I glance at the door as a reflex to see if anyone is looking in on us today.

We gather around after lecture to scan the grades from yesterday's test. As expected, I did poorly, but, having lowered my expectations, I'm surprisingly OK with it. All I care about is that passing is still statistically possible, and miraculously it somehow is. Any grade I get from here on out is fine, as long as I don't flunk out and have to do this again next summer.

I casually pick up a skull after lunch while we're waiting for afternoon classes to start. I've got no agenda here; I'm just holding the skull up to the light and examining it from different angles. On a whim, I open an anatomy atlas and look for a few of the features that we covered this morning.

While I'm killing some time with one skull, a new thought is forming inside my own. It's one of those moments when being older here is, at last, an advantage; when an old lesson makes a serendipitous reappearance. If engineers had a credo, it might be, "Don't agonize about the way things are: just work the problem." And paramedic school really built on that; our school motto was "improvise, adapt, and overcome."

OK, there are only two weeks left until our final. What if I was to come here every day, pick up a skull, find each of the 104 features, and let their intractable Latin names roll off my tongue? That could help. In the beginning, I could use the anatomy atlas as a guide, but, eventually, I would probably be able to perform my homage to the skull entirely from memory.

But wait! Why come in just *once* a day? That's for losers! How about a decidedly more compulsive *twice* a day? And what if I use a different skull each time? I don't know what will be on our final exam, but, if it's one of those features, I want to know the answer cold. It's worth a try.

I'm back in the apartment after class when Linda calls to tell me that she's on her way to our anniversary dinner. The actual date was last week, but, due to the ill-fated anatomy exam, we decided to postpone celebrating until tonight. We're meeting at Adornetto's, an Italian restaurant in Zanesville, about halfway between us.

Ninety minutes later, we're sitting comfortably at a small table with glasses of Chianti. It feels more like a date than it does our thirty-sixth wedding anniversary. We spend a delightful two hours together, talking, eating, drinking wine, and, especially, laughing. Anatomy has been left behind in another galaxy. It's one of those times I realize just how lucky I am and how rich my life really is. Daylight has given way to a warm summer evening by the time dinner ends. We hug one last time and convoy the few blocks back to the interstate, where she turns west, and I turn east.

I find an encouraging e-mail from Katie waiting for me when I get back. She shares some more memories of her time in veterinary school:

I remember learning about tons of holes in the skull (foramen this or that) and about names for lots of tiny parts of the skull that have fused together into one bone. What a pain!...At least you get to say cool words, like cribiform plate and pterygoid bone...Just think: you are almost done with anatomy!

Friday is a long and messy day in the lab. No more nice, dry skulls and plastic models for us; today we take a closer look at the real thing. With Mr. B's help, we use a bone saw to open George's skull and carefully remove its contents for study.

Later, it's time to leave for home with another week of classes behind me. Linda is rafting in Pennsylvania with friends, so I'll be there alone. I stop home just long enough to get the laundry started and then leave to meet our two sons at a local restaurant.

Fresh from another week on campus with my young friends, I'm sensitized to the difference between the relatively open conversations we have there and the more constrained ones I usually have here with Gary and Daniel. I understand why that is: the special nature of the father-son relationship and all that. I'll bet Sarge had different conversations with his sons than he did with us in the dorm. Still, tonight, I find myself wishing we could be more open.

Later Skyler and I relax on the couch in front of the TV while I keep the laundry moving and, still later, pay the bills. I realize while writing a check that I graduate exactly two years from today. That's six weeks down and 104 mysterious more of them to go.

Skyler nudges me awake in the morning. I feed him, put on some coffee, do some homework, and then go out for a haircut. I could get a haircut in Marietta, but I have had the same barber here for twenty years. Cassie has become a friend, and, through my monthly visits, we've kept up on each other's families. Like many friends, she wants to know what it's like living my particular version of what seems to be a common dream: suddenly doing something different with your life. She talks about going back to school herself one day, maybe when her ten-year-old son is grown.

I often run across people who, unlike Cassie, seem almost obligated to tell me why they couldn't possibly do anything as "brave" as I have. Actually my life hasn't involved much in the way of bravery. You really don't have to vault out of your comfort zone to make a change; it's surprisingly easy to try something new without abandoning your current life. My advice to people who ask: just try something new, even in a small way, if only to see how it makes you feel. In my case, a volunteer job one evening each week and, later, a night-school class were enough of a start.

Through such a series of small steps, the giant ocean liner that is your life slowly turns onto a new course. Speaking of nautical analogies, I've kept an old Irish fisherman's prayer on my bulletin board since the early days of my consulting business: "Dear God, have mercy on me! The sea is so wide and my boat is so small." I continue to be amazed how often the wind has caught my puny sails whenever I set out in a new direction.

It helps if the people closest to you are involved in your dream. Linda is often surprised when people tell me, "My wife would *never* let me do anything like that!" Her response: "Have they ever really asked?" Clearly marrying the right mate helps.

I spend a rare Saturday night in London, this time with the 2 Unit crew. When I started working here, only one other member of the department had ever gone to college. Others were interested but thought they were too old, an excuse that probably fell by the wayside when their second oldest member started taking prerequisites for PA school. Now Carla, our lieutenant tonight, is in nursing school, and others are planning their own adventures. It does put my recent anatomy debacles in perspective to think that maybe my example is encouraging others to take their own shots.

One of our runs tonight involves a man with abdominal pain. We've learned some new examination skills in school this week, and so I try to elicit what is called "Murphy's sign." I have the patient exhale and hold his breath while I press my hand under the right side of his rib cage. When I ask him to breathe in again, he stops abruptly when his inflamed gallbladder is pushed up against my hand.

"What did you just do?" Carla asks. I explain the skill and, in a small way, pay back some of the debt that I owe to all the EMS crews that have taught me over the years.

Sunday morning, after a three-hour drive, a hot shower, and a shave, I'm back to my books in Marietta. Linda and our friend Sally stop by later on their way home from rafting. They're animated as they recount being unceremoniously dumped into the New River. The apartment seems especially empty when they leave.

Marietta, Monday, August 9

There is just one week of anatomy left, and it starts with a long day working on the cranial nerves and structures of the eyes and neck. These features are small, but Team George has developed better dissection skills as the summer has rolled on.

I catch up on family happenings via e-mail, and everyone seems to be on the move. Katie and Tom are leaving for their last vacation "BK," or before kids. Daniel and a talk-show host from his station are back from Las Vegas. My parents are in New Jersey visiting my cousin, and Linda leaves soon for her aunt's memorial service in Charlotte. Family life spins on this year without me.

After a pleasant walk to campus on a clear, sixty-degree Tuesday morning, we take a short quiz, and then I go through the first of my two daily skull run-throughs. Jeff has noticed my new obsession and, drawing on a football metaphor, kids me good-naturedly about my "two-a-day" practices.

My weekdays are focused on schoolwork, letting me go home most weekends with no books and a clear conscience. I watch some TV during the week, mostly during dinner, and one show just before bedtime to clear my head. Rather than watching whatever happens to be on, I've decided to rent a digital video recorder from the cable company.

I'm back at the apartment for lunch just in time for the DVR installation. Surprise: the installer is the same grumpy guy who was supposed to have retired by now. Apparently he's still working—albeit part time—but no more cheerful than he was in June. He successfully installs my DVR between grumbles, and the apartment's aura brightens considerably once he leaves.

I study for the rest of the day, taking a break every now and then to sit on the front porch and watch rainstorms move through town. Later I get an e-mail from Tom, a friend and former client. A mutual colleague of ours had a heart attack and died yesterday on his way home from work. He had been on several of the project teams I worked with, and he always brought intensity and good humor to his work. Besides the usual thoughts at a time like this, his death at age fifty is a reminder that it's not a bad thing for me to be taking a shot at something new now, while I still can.

We study the tiny features of the inner ear on a rainy afternoon. Our summer with George is ending soon. We've saved all aspects of the dissection so that he and his colleagues can be cremated and honored at a memorial service next June. In spite of having studied his entire body, we really don't know much more about him than we did on our first day: age, occupation, and cause of death. We know he had a strong heart, but I can't help but wonder what these eyes saw during his eighty-six years and what prized memories were recorded in this brain.

I leave Friday after class for a short getaway before the final, getting home in time for a quiet dinner with Linda. After some errands on Saturday, it's time to pay the bills and update our finances. There have been a few changes since our last review, but, all in all, we're still more or less on track. Watching cash disappear from our bank account goes against my grain, but, so far, it hasn't bothered me as much as I might have predicted. Once you are committed to doing something, you just keep moving forward.

Sunday morning finds me on my way back to Marietta while Linda is off to walk in a park with our friends Joyce and Jeff. Probably by the time they're done, I'm back in the apartment, greeting my bonsai and unloading provisions. Other than making two trips to school for my reviews of the skull, I spend the day poring over notes and diagrams. The repetition seems to be working.

Marietta, Monday, August 16

The campus is alive for the first time this morning. It's the start of orientation week, and we're surrounded by gaggles of freshmen being led by upperclassman guides. I spot a sign announcing: "Welcome Class of 2008." Linda and I were in our university's class of 1968, so, forty years ago, I was going through my own orientation week.

The day before our orientation began, my friend and fellow freshman Bruce and I walked to the college dairy for ice cream. It was an especially hot afternoon, and we were sitting on a low brick wall eating ice-cream cones and talking about our adventures just ahead. We were just across the street from the university's coliseum, and suddenly its doors sprang open. What seemed like an endless procession of well-dressed young women filed out into the sun for the start of sorority rush. In keeping with the fashion of those times, each wore high heels and white gloves.

It was probably the first time that I laid eyes on Linda. We would meet in class a few weeks later, have an on-and-off relationship for four years, and marry six weeks after graduation. From then until now, I have lived closer to "happily ever after" than I had any right to expect.

Bruce would die nine years later, long after we lost track of each other among the 35,000 students on campus. Though forty years have gone by, I remember his friendship and that particular summer afternoon like it was this afternoon. Two friends who, moments earlier, were talking about their futures now sit transfixed, holding melting ice-cream cones and watching until the last white-gloved young woman disappears from sight.

Drew and I stop at the bookstore to pick up our fall-semester books. We enter a small room off the main store, where a woman takes our receipts for online purchases and wanders off to find our orders. While we wait, a young freshman enters and comes over to me.

"Excuse me, sir," he says, with great deference. "Can you help me find my textbooks?"

Drew starts laughing, and I have to smile. I tell the youngster that I'm a student, too, and that the clerk should be back to help him in a few minutes. Later Drew tells our classmates about the episode.

"Maybe it's time you joined a fraternity, like in *Old School*," Jeff suggests.

"You could be Old Blue," Seren offers, recalling the grizzled old navy veteran in the 2003 movie starring Will Ferrell, Vince Vaughn, and Luke Wilson.

I spend most of Tuesday studying from a master notebook of factoids that I doubt I could remember without further study. I make one pass through the notebook today and hope to make five more before Friday's test. On Wednesday, we have our last anatomy lecture, a review session, some case presentations, and our final lab with George. At last his earthly work is complete.

Linda calls and reports that she will soon be passing through the area on her way to her aunt's memorial service. She has a few minutes to spare for a quick dinner. Seeing her for a few minutes, even over the top of a fish sandwich, is an unexpected treat.

Thunderstorms rumble through town again just before dawn on Thursday, signaling the start of a day of total anatomy immersion. I take a break for lunch with Stan at the Third Street Deli before we both head to campus. Stan is looking for a place to study in an empty classroom with a whiteboard. For me, it's time for one of my last skull run-throughs. In spite of the gentle teasing I've been taking, the two-a-day sessions seem to be paying off. If you were to say, for example, "petrotympanic fissure," I could quickly point it out and tell you more about it than you would ever want to know.

Back at the apartment, I wander from room to room, each papered with diagrams from ADAM and the Netter's *Atlas of Human Anatomy*. I recite the twelve cranial nerves and their functions over and over: olfactory, optic, oculomotor, trochlear, trigeminal, abducens, facial, vestibulocochlear, glossopharangeal, vagus, accessory, and hypoglossal. It's a good thing I don't have a roommate.

During an after-dinner walk, I reflect on my summer and conclude that it's already been the experience of a lifetime. The work has been hard, but I enjoy the material, my classmates, and our instructors. I'm separated from family and friends, but weekend trips home, visitors, phone calls, and e-mails keep me connected.

I've also learned some things about myself—a real bonus at any age—including that I don't need an A in everything to prove that I made the right decision about coming here. A D is a failing grade in graduate school, but a good score tomorrow would get me a passing grade: a very low C. More importantly, it would give me the right to stay and see what happens next. That is all that really matters.

Our test starts at noon, but I'm up well before dawn to resume my wanderings through the apartment, where I recite the names of nerves, bones, and muscles, as if lecturing to invisible students. Finally I'm out the door with a garbage bag of anatomy clothes slung over my shoulder for what, I hope, will be their last outing.

The fates—and the faculty—must be smiling today, because, as the test questions spool by, I feel that I'm doing OK. There are some bonus questions, and many of my 104 skull features lurk among them. I walk out of the building hopeful that I got what I need to stay here. Beyond that, I'll make no predictions.

I clean the apartment and pack for a ten-day break between terms. Grades aren't back yet, and maybe I'm jumping the gun, but I feel that it's time to live out a summerlong fantasy. Into the plastic garbage bag one last time go the faded shirt, stained pants, frayed belt, and no-longer-white sneakers. I walk out into the parking lot behind the apartment. Using one hand to shield my eyes from the summer sun, I sling the plastic bag high and watch it tumble end over end, landing in the far corner of the dumpster with a satisfying thud.

A few days later, I'm back in Westerville when I get an e-mail from Penny. I won't need to replace my discarded anatomy clothes after all. Surprisingly I did well enough on the test to get a middle C for my roller coaster of a term. Nice enough, but, more importantly, I won't be repeating anatomy next summer. None of us will. We're all moving on together into the new semester.

No more two-a-days. Anatomy boot camp is over. Let's just see what happens next.

CHAPTER 9

CLOSE TO HOME

Westerville, Sunday, August 29

U nless you're a teacher, summer breaks are something you merely watch your children have. No sleeping in late for you; somebody has to go out and make some money. These past ten days have been my first summer break in decades. Unlike some of the earlier ones, I didn't get a summer job laying water lines or collecting stream-flow data. I did get to spend most of it with family and friends. Daniel and I have one of our long-delayed lunches together. A dose of his cheerfulness and optimism always does me good.

And, with no studying to do, there's time for a few extra shifts on the squad. One evening starts with the usual banter around the table over a tasty meatloaf dinner. Later we adjourn to the driveway to lounge, talk, and eat rocky-road ice cream. Nights on the squad clearly aren't for the diet-conscious.

Our sleep is interrupted several times, usually for complaints like chest pain, but one call breaks the mold. An intoxicated man has driven his pickup into a woman's house. Fortunately no one is hurt, and the driver ran away, cleverly leaving his truck protruding from the living room, its rear license plate clearly visible in our lights. Sheriff's deputies find him a short time later, sleeping it off in a nearby ditch.

On one of my evenings at home, Linda and I man a booth for the Otterbein Lake park project. The park was her idea and, over the years, she has won grants, recruited volunteers, and obtained city approvals. I'm proud of all that she's done, but, now, I'm mostly worried about her health.

We learn that premalignant cells are the cause of her bleeding, and she needs a total hysterectomy. She wants it done as soon as possible; recovery will take some time, and she is determined to hold our grandson when he's born in November. Our family is coming to the rescue, with Gary and his wife planning to stay at our house to help out. I'll have to be flexible, staying home when needed and keeping up with my studies when I can.

Back on campus, while we were gone for our break, undergraduate students moved in for the fall term. Having been through many move-in days myself—and from both sides of those nervous good-bye hugs—it's easy to picture families moving boxes into new dorm rooms with high hopes and more than a little anxiety.

Many aspects of the dormitory experience have probably changed over the last forty years. My circa-1960s dorm room—located in a reasonably new building at the time—could support radios and stereos, along with the odd immersion heater for individual cups of really bad instant coffee. It couldn't handle the microwave ovens of the day, let alone air conditioners, and most dorms only had televisions in common areas. As for personal mailboxes, we just had the snail-mail kind. No one would have had a clue what dot-com means.

Modern dorms are different; the rooms are Internet ready, with enough power for computers, refrigerators, microwaves, televisions, and whatever else you might like to pick up at Best Buy. Women, especially, are organized enough to contact their roommates in advance, deciding on color schemes and who will be bringing which appliances to campus.

Most dorms have been coed for some time. Back in my day, women were allowed in—officially anyway—only for special events, like Homecoming Day. That was until one of my more resourceful dorm mates discovered that there was no official university definition for what "special event" meant. From then on, he filled out the paperwork, so every weekend became *special* for those of us in Cambridge A. I can't recall his name now, but I'd like to think he went on to become a really successful lawyer.

Regardless of the impressive technical and social differences between then and now, I suspect Marietta College's latest group of dorm rats will go through the same rites of passage that we did. Living alone for the first time, making friends, learning that not everyone thinks like you do, and finding your own special path to adulthood.

My first Monday back brings a new ambiance to the campus. The parking lots are full and unfamiliar students pass me in the hallways. But our classroom is full of familiar faces as Gloria welcomes us back and introduces the new term.

Unlike our summer of anatomy immersion, the fall semester looks more traditional. Classes will last most of the day, and we'll sit in one spot while instructors shuttle in and out. I suspect that, by the end of the term, the front-row seat I so casually picked out in June will be completely molded to my shape. Because of the nature of our training—all Tuesdays, for example, won't always be the same—schedules for the next few weeks have been left in our mailboxes.

Bathroom breaks have been built into the schedule, and we're told to wait for them. Having older plumbing than my comrades, I'll have to ignore that advice when necessary. I try not to be different from my classmates, but, in some ways, I guess I just am. I've also gotten permission to ignore the keep-your-mobile-phone-off rule. Mine stays on vibrate because of Linda's upcoming surgery and Katie's pregnancy, along with having other children and elderly parents to keep tabs on.

Preliminaries behind us, it's time to get things going. Throwing out the first pitch will be Dr. Peter Hogan, who will be our physiology professor. Jan whispers to me that, as an undergraduate, she was afraid of him. Just as she finishes her story, a tall, imposing man in his early sixties, with a booming voice and a strong New England accent, strides into the room.

Dr. Hogan puts down a forty-four-ounce plastic drink cup and warmly welcomes us. He seems genuinely happy to be here. Perhaps it was just his size and voice that scared Jan. He'll be covering the functions of the body's many systems this term. That's a lot to learn, but hopefully I can build mental models of how things work, rather than having to memorize more isolated facts.

Dr. Hogan lectures from multicolor PowerPoint slides displayed on a large screen by a projector mounted to the ceiling. Educational tools certainly have come a long way. During my freshman year, our math professor lectured to 300 of us from the stage of a large auditorium. Using a grease pencil, he slowly wrote equations onto an endless roll of clear plastic. His only-somewhat legible scratches were projected onto a very small screen at the front of the hall.

Besides larger, clearer, and more colorful instructional materials, we have other advantages now. Our lecturers will bring in their elaborate presentations on small flash drives, leaving electronic copies that we can retrieve. My classmates from the 1960s would marvel and approve.

OLD MAN ON CAMPUS

Dr. Hogan starts his lecture today by delving into cellular processes. Comparing what we now know about cells with what we knew when I first took biology is like comparing a modern map of the world with one drawn during the Middle Ages. Old maps sometimes labeled what wasn't then known with the phrase, "There be dragons." My high school biology textbook said, more or less, "There be cytoplasm." Knowing more now somehow makes cells seem even more mysterious. It also makes me wish I could come back to a classroom in a few hundred years to see what's new.

Dr. Hogan comes over as I gather my books to leave. "Barry," he asks, "how does it feel to be in class with students when you're as old as their parents?"

"I really don't feel that out of place," I reply. "I'm enjoying it." I don't add that I'm also older than most of those parents.

"Glad to hear it," he says. "How old are you?"

"Fifty-eight," I answer. "And you?"

"Sixty-two." Dr. Hogan will be the only professor I'll have this year who is older than I am.

I'm in the apartment warming up some soup for lunch when Linda calls. Her surgery has been scheduled for tomorrow morning. She sounds calm, but we're both nervous. I pack to leave right after class and send e-mails to my professors. I won't be in class tomorrow, and I'll be playing it by ear after that for a while.

The highlight of the afternoon is Tim's lecture on physical examination techniques. He tells us that, in this age of modern tests, we sometimes forget what we can learn about a patient just by looking, listening, and touching. He also clears up one concern: just how much looking, listening, and touching will involve our classmates. We learn that, yes, for the most part, we'll be examining each other, however, paid patients will be brought in for the more intimate exams. That's a relief.

Linda and I are at Mount Carmel St. Ann's Hospital at half past five the next morning. It's the same place where I started my medical career as a volunteer twenty years ago. The admissions clerk asks me what I do for a living. After hearing my answer, she puts me down as "unemployed." Not what I would have chosen, but so be it.

Linda's surgery starts at half past six. I try to study while waiting for news, but I can't concentrate. All I can do is walk around the hospital and try to find some coffee. I run into my podiatrist in a hallway. Talking with Dr. Dave for a few minutes relieves some of the pressure.

Eventually Linda is wheeled back to her room, looking gray and without her usual spark. Though I've seen her deliver three babies and go through other surgeries, until now, I couldn't actually picture her really ill. All I can do now is hold her hand. After a while, she starts talking in short, monotone phrases. Her surgeon drops by to report that he saw nothing out of the ordinary and that the pathology report should be ready by the end of the week. It's time to take a breath.

Linda is weak and queasy but slowly improves throughout the afternoon. I stay in her room, building a makeshift bed in the corner to spend the night. She gets stronger toward morning, eventually asking for the narcotics to be stopped. She gets an argument from her nurse, but she prevails. You don't get far arguing with a Wilson woman. She starts to feel better almost immediately, celebrating with an early-morning breakfast of water, ice chips, and a saltine.

"Would you like me to stay here today?" I ask.

"No," she answers. "Go back to school. I'll see you tonight."

It's still dark, and traffic is light on the interstate. I'm tired but mostly just relieved and grateful. I didn't expect things to go wrong, but—even after only two months of PA school—I'm intensely aware that they could have.

Back at my apartment, there's just enough time for a shower and an English muffin before lectures start. Jan recorded yesterday's lectures for me, and there are also paper handouts and PowerPoint files that I can catch up with. Fortunately it's still early in the term, so it's hard to fall too far behind.

I'm back at the hospital by the end of the day, where I find Linda has been getting steadily stronger. I stay with her until bedtime, and then, rather than driving back to Marietta, I decide to sleep in my own bed at home. Our dog is at Katie's for the duration, so the house is quiet. Maybe the cat is glad to see me, but, then again, it's not easy to know what a cat thinks about anything.

I'm out of the house well before sunrise in yesterday's clothes and back on the road. Once again, there's just time for a hot shower, a change of clothes, and a quick breakfast in the apartment before another day of classes. Then it's back to the hospital in time to talk to the surgeon during his evening rounds.

I find Linda feeling better and starting to eat regular food. The surgeon stops by to talk about her care over the next few weeks. I ask him a question, and it's a moment I don't think I'll ever forget. He silently looks me in the eye for several seconds with no expression on his face. After failing to acknowledge my question—let alone answer it—he slowly turns back to Linda. I hope I'm never that rude as a clinician.

I drive back to Marietta when visiting hours end, making my third one-way trip of the day. All this driving has given me more than enough time to catch up on the recorded lectures. Other than losing some sleep and getting to know the inside of the car better than I would care to, it has all been good. Linda is OK, I was with her for the surgery and every evening since, and I've made it through the first week of the term.

I'm home Friday evening after my eighth one-way trip of the week. I retrieve Skyler from Tom and Katie's and come home to find Linda relaxing comfortably on the couch. Our pack is reunited and on the mend.

CHAPTER 10

STORM CLOUDS

Marietta, Monday, September 6

Like the Fourth of July, this sunny and warm Labor Day is just another day of class for us. Stan, though, has a visitor. His older sister Ginia has driven out from Colorado in a pickup that will replace the car he borrowed to get here. I join them for dinner and quickly learn that Ginia shares Stan's sense of humor. She says she's here to "check on my baby brother."

I learn more about their family over dinner. Ginia and Stan's father emigrated from China and supported his family by working long hours in a succession of restaurants. He eventually started his own, with his family working by his side. He died a few years ago, and their mother has since remarried. Now Ginia is the glue holding the family together. She is very close to Stan and has mobilized their friends to help him out.

When we're alone, Ginia thanks me for "looking out for my baby brother." Actually Stan probably does more for me than the other way around. I enjoy his friendship and look forward to the tapping at my door that signals his usually unexpected arrival. And it's hard not to crack a smile whenever I see him.

When Stan does stop by, he is usually on his way home from a late-day run, studying alone in an empty classroom, or playing online games in the computer lab. His ease in his own skin, coupled with a prodigious appetite for playing computer games, has led some of the faculty to suspect that he is not taking his training seriously. I know that is not the case at all.

Lately, he's been talking about the recent influx of business students on campus from China. They mostly keep to themselves, and, in spite of their common heritage, Stan has not yet been able to make a connection. He refers to them as "coming from the Source."

We stop at Stan's apartment on the way back from dinner. I've never been here before, and it's hard to miss the large pile of empty shipping boxes. Marietta has private garbage collection, and Stan—close enough to the financial edge as it is—doesn't want to pay the fee. Before he is crushed by his own trash, I suggest that it could find a home in the dumpster behind my apartment. Later, his truck glides into my lot with its lights off, and we conspiratorially unload the contraband.

Tuesday starts with our first pathophysiology lecture from Dr. Joe Kruger. He works part-time as a hospital pathologist and often lectures via Internet video, as he is doing this morning. His course will cover some of the many ways things can go wrong with the exquisite human processes Dr. Hogan has begun to describe. When he lectures from out of town, Dr. Kruger first has to find an empty hospital conference room with an Internet connection. Judging from the whiteboard behind him today, this one must have recently hosted a Bible study.

On Jan's recommendation, I stop at Izzy's, a small snack bar in a nearby campus building, during our mid-morning break. There I make a surprising discovery: this college actually provides free popcorn. Also, for a fee, pretty good coffee and Krispy Kreme donuts. I skip the donuts and spend an hour in the sun with a muffin and coffee. With the undergraduates back on campus in full force, I can see why some people like to teach. Having animated young people around you probably makes most days feel like spring.

Linda sounds stronger tonight on the phone. She is moving around the house easily, and, after three months of living alone, she enjoys having Gary and his wife stay with her. If she feels up to it, she'll visit me this weekend for Marietta's Sternwheel Festival.

Stan and I meet after dinner to finish a homework assignment. We videotape each other gathering information for a complete History and Physical, or H&P in medical lingo. We take turns playing the patient, and we're free to make up our answers. I pretty much play it straight when Stan is asking the questions, but all bets are off when it's his turn to be the pretend patient. He gamely plays the role of a drug-addicted unfortunate with many homosexual partners and multiple diseases. With role-playing over, we partake in some video golf at the Student Union before heading back to our apartments.

Our class has started working on group projects involving alternative medicine. Stan, Jan, and I are preparing a presentation on Reiki, an ancient healing art involving gentle massage and deep relaxation. Sean, an engineering classmate of mine from forty years ago, is now an expert Reiki practitioner. He would be a great resource for our project. I just don't happen to know where he is right now.

It's still easy for me to picture Sean at twenty-one, a smile on his face while smoking big cigars in our engineering honor-society lounge. He would be cracking jokes in his thick Baltimore accent and talking about his dream of one day owning an Alfa Romeo. Sean married his college sweetheart after graduation, went to work as a microwave engineer, and later found a job on the West Coast. Along the way, he and his wife had two children, and their marriage eventually came to an end. He did get his Alfa, but it was in the shop more often than not and eventually disposed of.

In spite of some disappointments along the way, Sean was his old ebullient self the last time we spoke. He has gone through his own metamorphosis from engineering to medicine, and now he's out there somewhere. I send him an e-mail tonight, asking about his current life and Reiki. I hope that my electronic note in a bottle finds him happy and well.

I wake up Wednesday to the sound of an unusually heavy rain drumming on the cars outside my bedroom window. The clock radio announces that a remnant of Hurricane Frances is passing through town, and heavy rains will continue for the next few days. Just a few blocks away, the Ohio River now stands a comfortable twenty feet below flood stage, but that could be changing soon.

Given the weather, I decide to drive to school, where our focus today is on handling difficult patients. I've had my share as a paramedic—usually because of intoxication, a head injury, or low blood sugar—but never anything like what Tim is describing today. Some patients will swamp us with more complaints than we can handle in one visit. He advises us to have them pick their top three problems for the day. Others may even come on to us sexually. We might need to get a chaperone, give the patient a stern warning, or arrange for a different health-care provider to see them in the future.

The rain continues Thursday, and, surprisingly, the Ohio now stands only five feet below flood stage. The river has reclaimed the first rank of trees on its banks, but the Sternwheel Festival is still on for this weekend. Several stern-wheelers are already in port, and carloads of tourists are arriving.

Most of our class has started a new Thursday-night tradition of going out to dinner as a group before our weekly evening lecture. Tonight we're at the Harmar, partaking of the half-price prime-rib special. We get ten ounces of surprisingly good prime rib, a salad, and a baked potato for just ten dollars. Dr. Bauer, a professor in the school of education, teaches this course, which is designed to help graduate students prepare for their thesis research. The rain starts up again as we leave his lecture.

By Friday morning, the river is only eighteen inches below flood stage, so the festival's midway has been moved back a block from the waterfront, just in case. Runoff from thousands of square miles to our north and east continues to flow by silently, just a hundred feet away.

After Dr. Hogan's lecture on the genetics of disease, we have the first test of our fledgling physical-examination skills. We are paired with class-mates and take turns being examiners and patients. When it's our turn to be the examiner, we go through the steps we've learned while a faculty member grades our performance. After three months of bonding, we try to help each other as best we can. As patients, we're like baseball managers, using every sly, nonverbal signal we can think of to help nervous examiners remember the next step.

When school ends for the week, Linda, Gary, and I meet in a McDonald's parking lot halfway between Marietta and home. Linda looks more like her old self now, and her smile brightens my day. The Sternwheel Festival is well underway when we get back to town. Marietta is a busy place on this warm fall evening. Besides the stern-wheelers tied up in port, there are many food booths and craft exhibits. One end of First Street has been turned into a stage. We set our camp chairs in the middle of the street and listen as a country band starts to play. It feels like we could live here forever.

Saturday morning reminds me of one of the many bed-and-breakfast trips we've taken over the years. This time we just happen to be in a small town that is having its annual river festival. There is one important difference: I have work to do. Linda reads while I do homework and pay bills. We go to a class party later at Aaron and Liz's condo, where, when the sky darkens, we watch festival fireworks over the harbor.

Marietta, Monday, September 13

My first challenge this morning is finding something clean to wear. Somehow I have ended up with lots of clean shirts, but no clean Levi's. I settle on a pair of Dockers, only to have Aaron ask me why I'm so dressed up today. I guess that wearing business casual to college is like wearing a tuxedo anywhere else.

We're continuing to learn new physical-examination techniques. Today, it's percussing, or placing the finger of one hand flat on your patient while you strike it with the tip of the index finger of your other hand. With practice, you can interpret the reflected sound to determine whether you're directly over a structure filled mostly with air, fluid, or tissue.

We seem to go through three stages as we learn new medical skills. First we learn the basic mechanics, then how to perform the skill on a routine basis, and, finally, how to do it effortlessly enough to inspire your patient's confidence. In other words, making it look like you've been doing it your whole life. Some people move through these stages and skills faster than others.

I remember how, as a new EMT, I tried to get comfortable taking blood pressures. One night, I had trouble taking a firefighter's blood pressure on the scene of a hazardous-materials spill. Try as I might, I couldn't hear his pulse over all the heavy equipment noise. I still cringe when I remember him getting a paramedic buddy to take over, pointing at me as he scoffed, "He thinks I'm dead!"

There was, however, a pleasant postscript to that long-ago evening. When the incident finally ended early the next morning, the incident commander led our procession of emergency vehicles to a local bakery, where he knew that warm cherry pastries would be coming out of the oven at precisely five o'clock. In EMS, you've got to be ready for anything in the middle of the night, whether it's trying to take a blood pressure, getting scoffed at, or eating the odd warm Danish.

Some of the skills we're learning now involve new instruments. We've been issued otoscopes for looking in ears and ophthalmoscopes for eyes. The ophthalmoscope is, by far, the most mysterious tool we've seen. With only two controls, it's deceptively simple: one control sets viewer magnification and the other light intensity. More light should mean you can see more, but that's usually not the case. Instead, the patient tears up more quickly and has to blink.

We've been taught how to hold the ophthalmoscope against our eye and then slowly move along an oblique path toward the patient's eye. We're first supposed to see the "red reflex," which is the red glow you sometimes see in flash photos, especially of small children. Then we're supposed to move in closer, find the blood vessels of the retina, and then follow them back to the optic disk. It sounds easy, as far as the physical steps go, and I think I could play a convincing PA doing an eye exam on TV. Unfortunately, while it might look like I knew what I was doing, I would probably see nothing.

And time after time, nothing is exactly what I see. But even a blind dog occasionally finds a bone, and, once in a while, I do, too. This afternoon, while Stan patiently stands with his eyes wide open and tearing, I briefly glimpse the vessels of his retina. Just as I do, the light is finally too much for him, and he has to blink and turn away. I practice later, back at the apartment, looking at paper clips on my mantle. It helps me figure out the right magnification setting, but paper clips don't blink. Mastering this skill is going to take a while.

I run into Seren on my after-dinner walk this evening. He's more or less being dragged along by Duke, his new and extremely energetic dog. Come to think of it, their personalities match perfectly. Both are enthusiastic, athletic, and more than a little interested in the ladies of their respective species. Seren pauses for just an instant before Duke pulls him off in a new direction.

I get an e-mail reply tonight from Sean, my temporarily misplaced old friend and Reiki expert. He's attached an excellent paper on Reiki and also brings me up to date on his life. His message comes from the skeleton of a hotel he's building in a small town in Brazil, where he works with a local spiritualist healer. I try to picture him, typing away on his laptop under the stars in a partially framed building. Given the chance, lives can move in unpredictable directions.

Our class is starting up a coed flag football team, and I've been thinking about playing. I was an enthusiastic—if mediocre—intramural athlete forty years ago. Our team back then was no great shakes either. Then again, how good would you expect a football team from the honors dorm to be? I was thirty pounds lighter in those days and could eat five McDonald's hamburgers, fries, and a chocolate shake for lunch without gaining an ounce. While I weighed considerably less than a real defensive end, I enjoyed the chance to rush the quarterback and try to cut off runs to the outside.

My thoughts about playing football again run into reality when I meet Stan on my way to class. He hyperextended his knee at practice last night. Watching him wince with every step convinces me that my contact-sports career is over.

Our day begins with a physiology lecture and then moves on to new physical-examination skills. We're learning how to examine skin, hair, and nails. These skills have an antique, yet practical, flavor. Indian scouts used to look for clues on the trail from hoofprints and bent twigs. Now we're being taught that spoon-shaped nails can indicate an iron deficiency or an underactive thyroid, while whitish nails might suggest cirrhosis of the liver. We also have many pages of skin lesions to learn, complete with full-color illustrations. That I can look at pictures like these while eating dinner is testimony to how desensitized I'm becoming.

I'm back at school after dinner to watch our intramural football team's first game. We call ourselves Team Dartos, after the tough, muscular layer of tissue covering the scrotum. Clearly our summer of anatomy had some nonacademic benefits. There is considerable talent on the field tonight, and even more enthusiasm. Several classmates were athletic training majors and are still in good shape.

Seren, a former college rugby player, plays football pretty much the way he lives. He is wearing an unpadded leather rugby helmet and throwing himself around like he's indestructible. Kevin was a lineman on Marietta's football team, and I can still see his love for the game—and the chance to get physical again. Julia, a former college soccer player, runs like a bull, often dragging defenders who hang on for dear life while they reach for her flag.

Watching the proceedings from the sidelines with our subs makes me feel like a parent watching his kids. My classmates share the feeling; Michelle asks me if I've brought the sliced oranges, the typical halftime snack parents bring to their children's soccer games.

I've spent many an evening like this, watching my own kids play soccer or baseball. Along the way, I've eaten plenty of hot dogs for dinner while sitting in a lawn chair, still in my work clothes. Some of those games are preserved on bulky videocassettes stacked in our front closet. Every child would get a trophy at the end of the season, even though you would need a magnifying glass to read the words on the ninth-place statuette. Our children have grown up and moved away, but some of those trophies are still in our basement.

Team Dartos beats the Raging Mullets 35-21 tonight, coming off the field with its enthusiasm and sense of humor intact. The evening makes me miss my kids all the more, and I call each of them when I get back to the apartment.

Dr. Kruger gets things started Thursday with a lecture on Down's syndrome, followed by a quiz. Afterward, I decide to try out the newly remodeled main cafeteria for lunch, and Jan comes along. Once inside, we find a posted list showing different prices for students, parents, visitors, faculty, and so on. Once you pay, you can go inside and eat whatever you would like.

The student cashier looks up and sees a man in his late fifties accompanied by a young woman in her twenties. "Excuse me, sir," she asks sweetly. "Are you a parent?" Here we go again. Well, I suppose I don't look very much like Jan's date, or her baby brother here to see big sis's school.

"Yes, I am," I reply. "Just not hers. I'm a student, too."

We pay our five bucks and enter a large, modern area. Other than the swarm of students, this doesn't resemble the college cafeteria of my past at all. There is no mystery meat to identify, nor poorly refrigerated milk to test for curdling in hot coffee before you would dare put it on your cereal. There are multiple food stations here. One holds a Mongolian barbecue, another a large salad bar, another assorted pizzas, and, still another, steak fajitas. And, of course, there is a large dessert bar. Clearly this will be my big meal of the day.

After lunch, the class talks about the physician assistant's role in various types of medical practices. At this stage, I'm interested in emergency, family, or internal medicine. Hopefully my clinical rotations next year will clear things up for me.

The heavy rains that have dogged us for days begin anew on Friday morning. This time, it's the remnant of our second hurricane of the season, and the river is once again on the rise. That I'm paying attention to a river's stage for the first time in my life is something of a curiosity to me.

I pack my car for my weekly trip home and drive to class in the downpour. My usual parking lot is full, so I park a few blocks away. I have to cross a small footbridge over what is usually just a trickle of water running in a small ditch to get to class. It's a raging creek this morning, water coursing rapidly just a few inches below my feet.

The heavy rain continues all day. By the time I reach the footbridge again, it's covered with flowing water, and the creek is well out of its banks. The water also has claimed much of the surrounding grassland and is lapping close to a nearby dorm. I find another route back to my car. Leaving town for the weekend, I'm oblivious to what five inches of new rain is doing to an already soggy town.

CHAPTER 11

THE GREAT FLOOD

Westerville, Saturday, September 18

I'm safely home in Westerville, but the Ohio River is four feet above flood stage in Marietta and still rising. Cars in some campus parking lots have disappeared beneath the muddy water, and the football stadium has flooded. By the time the rain finally stops on Sunday, the river is an astounding ten feet above flood stage, and Marietta is in the national news.

The sun is out again, but there still is the potential for more damage as the large watershed to the north and east of town continues to drain. Stan calls to let me know the campus will be closed for at least a week. Several dorms have been flooded, and residents are being moved to higher ground.

Our classroom building wasn't damaged, and our program doesn't keep to the same schedule as the rest of the college. I'm not really sure if we'll have classes or not, and I also wonder how my friends are faring. I decide to drive to Marietta, taking old clothes and a shovel with me just in case.

A state trooper motions for me to stop as I approach the outskirts of town. The road ahead is closed, and he gives me a map showing an alternate route. I find my apartment high and dry. The floodwaters would probably have had to be forty feet higher to be lapping at my door. I begin exploring the town on foot and start to encounter water about halfway to campus. The Third Street Deli is washed out, along with the barbershop next door. I wonder when the friendly woman behind the deli counter will be able to get back to work.

While there is no water around our classroom building, the street out front is flooded. My usual parking lot is under water, and any cars left there are completely submerged. I watch a canoe full of students paddle by. Gloria is standing on dry land in front of our building, snapping pictures of the unconventional boaters. She confirms that classes have been cancelled for the week.

I walk downtown, where mud stains on the brick walls show a high watermark that would have been up to my armpits. People in canoes paddle by flooded stores on Front Street as if they were shoppers in Venice. Brownies Market, home of our much-beloved pepperoni rolls, is ruined. Water is also running into the basement of the Lafayette Hotel. A passerby tells me that the Harmar Tavern, with its prized bologna sandwiches, is also out of action.

Stan's apartment is completely surrounded by water; he has put up a sign, renaming the place Stan's Island, in his front window. Several of our classmates have left town. Aaron and Liz's condo, just across a small road from the Ohio River, has taken a real beating. The water rose well into their second story and their two cars were destroyed in the garage. Aaron has pictures of looters arriving in boats from across the river.

After wandering around town for a few hours, I head back to Westerville for an unscheduled week off. I'm safe and dry at home, but life in Marietta is still very much up in the air. Jan's emails keep us refugees posted. It's not known when—or if—Brownie's Market and the Harmar Tavern will reopen. Besides being keenly interested in future sources of pepperoni rolls and fried-bologna sandwiches, we've come to know the people working there, and we wonder what will become of them.

The crackle of official college e-mail paints a picture of life for those who've remained on campus. A temporary bus station is being set up and emergency loans given to those who still want to leave town. Those who remain are being asked to help the city clean up but to stay off the streets after eight o'clock at night due to a general curfew. A local church is conducting a "Laundry Ministry" to help keep students clean while they work. The water finally dips back below flood stage on Tuesday. Jan reports:

> The problem now is the devastation. The dorms on Fourth Street were torn apart and cleaned today as much as possible, but some of the rooms would make anyone sick to their stomach...

Reconstruction continues throughout the week. The county health department is busy debunking rumors of a possible hepatitis risk from the floodwaters. Even though the college plans to start up again next week, it doesn't sound like life will be back to normal anytime soon. Loans are being made to those whose textbooks were destroyed. Some dorms need extensive rehabilitation, so—for a few weeks at least—residents will be staying in motels on the outskirts of town.

Stan abandons his apartment for a time and joins me in Westerville, where we do research for our theses. He returns to Marietta later and e-mails his own assessment:

> Everything seems pretty cool now. Your apartment was never really in danger of swimming so I don't think anything is wrong on Fourth Street. I, on the other hand, have not had hot water in five days. I don't like cold showers.

> I ran into the older gal who usually is behind the counter [at Brownies] at the Walmart. According to her, they are closing. Who knows, maybe there is still hope. FEMA, help!!!

By Saturday, it sounds like life is starting to return to normal. The *Marietta Times* website reports:

> For days, people have asked whether Brownie's Donut and Pastry Shop at 258 Front St. will close. Owners there say their immediate plans are to get back on their feet. The same goes for Rossi Pasta, 114 Greene St., whose back door opens to the Ohio River Levee. Rumors that business will close are untrue, managers say.

> No downtown or Pike Street business has confirmed it's closing, and most have worked hard to do business once again.

Our family gathers on Sunday to celebrate Linda's birthday. We do her day up right with cake, ice cream, candles, pictures, presents, plastic leis, cone-shaped party hats for everyone—including the dog—and plenty of laughter. There should be a new grandson here with us in time for our next family party.

My unscheduled vacation is over when the party ends. By the time I return to Marietta, most of the city has dried out, with only a few isolated puddles and clumps of drying mud left to show where water once had been. Other than some closed dorms and fraternity houses, the campus looks like nothing happened. Our merry band of twenty-one is back in town, and classes start again tomorrow morning.

CHAPTER 12

THE SHORT WHITE COAT

Marietta, Monday, September 27

It's the first day back after what is already being called the Great Flood. There is an all-campus meeting after dinner to discuss how to help the community recover. I pass a small puddle in the darkness on my way home. The last liquid remnant of the Great Flood lies in front of a Third Street law office.

Tuesday is supposed to start with Dr. Kruger's lecture via Internet, but we can't get his video feed to come up on our monitor. The engineer in me—or maybe just the old junior high audiovisual geek—wonders what's wrong. After the class is released, Gloria and I trace wires and eventually find one that's loose.

Speaking of junior high behavior, I'm growing self-conscious about being the one in class who always asks the most questions. No one here has said anything to me about it, but, on refection, I realize that it has been one of my traits for quite some time. When I was young, Mom encouraged me in this, her theory being that if I had questions in class, then others probably did, too. My interrogation techniques were honed further by jobs that involved making and listening to presentations in dimly lit rooms while everyone drank entirely too much coffee. In that culture, you were expected to ask all the questions you wanted to until you had all the answers you needed.

I'm once again spending my days listening to presentations, and, even though I know the culture here is different, I still ask lots of questions. I should be old enough not to worry about how I'm perceived by others, but I have to admit that it's on my mind.

With Mom, my question-asking role model.

I enjoy the walk to campus on a sunny, cool Wednesday morning for lectures on the immune system. We regroup after lunch in shorts and T-shirts to practice our physical-examination skills. We pair up this time to examine each other's eyes, ears, and thyroid glands.

It's hard for me not to feel at least a little self-conscious when it's my turn to be examined. My body does, after all, show a bit more wear and tear than anyone else here. Come to think of it, I probably should get a tuition discount for being a part-time teaching aid. Today my partner discovers wax in my right ear. Fortunately that is more a matter of genetics than cleanliness. At least I remembered to shave my ears.

Dr. Bauer, our Thursday-night instructor, is an excellent storyteller. My appreciation for that grew recently when I learned that he was born deaf. It must have taken him a great deal of effort to get where he is today. He teaches with great flair and is a favorite of many of the students.

"You probably didn't know this," he announces tonight, "but I hold the southeast Ohio record for killing deer...with my car. The record, incidentally, is seven."

The class starts to chuckle. The area around Marietta is rural and wooded and a destination for deer hunters. Ohio has different deer-hunting seasons for bows, muzzleloaders, and conventional guns. Even with our concealed-carry law, there isn't a season for automobiles, even if you have a musket in your trunk.

Dr. Bauer apparently improves his odds with frequent early-morning trips to Columbus. This time he had just started for the Columbus airport with his daughter when Bambie number seven sprinted in front of his car. Hitting a deer at sixty-five miles per hour got the immediate attention of passing motorists, and at least one called 9-1-1.

The responding squad strapped Dr. Bauer and his daughter to back-boards as a precaution and brought them to the hospital for evaluation. Fortunately, beyond a few bumps and bruises, neither one was seriously injured. As he recounts this part of the story, Dr. Bauer lies down on a table at the front of the lecture hall, legs cantilevered over the edge as if he were lying on a backboard. His comedic delivery is impeccable, and the class howls with laughter.

We have a physical-examination test Friday, and I'm paired with Jan. When the time comes to look into her eyes with my ophthalmoscope, I do it by the book, but I still don't see anything of those wily retinal blood vessels. One day soon, I hope it will click. For now, though, I just describe what I'm doing and pretend to find the still-elusive features. We get a critique later by e-mail:

> Everyone needs to get closer for the eye exam...The oral cavity is a dark cave without a light; use yours...Your patient has given you permission to do the exams by sitting in the room. You should let them know what you are doing so as not to startle them, but you don't need to ask permission again...Overall, everyone did a very good job...you will get faster.

My weekend starts in London, this time with the 3 Unit crew. Our night is true to the tenant of EMS lore that says, if you're tired at the start of your shift, it's almost guaranteed that the so-called run gods will keep you out of bed all night. One of our many runs tonight is for Sandy, a forty-something-year-old woman who—unlike us—can be found in bed.

We get the details from her sister and brother-in-law, as Sandy's young son sits in his aunt's lap. Apparently Sandy had been in her bedroom when she suddenly reappeared to tell them that she had taken "all" of her medications. Then she kissed each of them good-bye and calmly went back to bed. This touching family scene provoked the call to 9-1-1.

Fortunately we find Sandy still conscious and willing to answer questions. The police stand by while she admits to having had three beers tonight, along with approximately ten tablets each of heart and anxiety medications. She had tried this before, and tonight is particularly despondent because her estranged husband is trying to take away their son. I guess we know what his grounds might be.

Given her actions, she has no choice about what's going to happen next, and we begin packaging her for a trip to the hospital. She wants to know where we're taking her. I tell her that it will be the local hospital, just a few minutes away. "I don't want to go *there*!" she retorts. "They won't do *anything* for me!"

Reflecting on her recent behavior, my partner whispers in my ear, "You'd think that would be *just* where she would want to go!" I explain to Sandy that the hospital she prefers is too far away for someone in her condition.

Sandy becomes progressively less responsive. We move her to our truck, where we start an IV and give her naloxone to reverse the effects of any narcotics she may have neglected to tell us about. We also give her oxygen and IV fluids to counteract a drop in blood pressure. Sandy is stable en route to the hospital, where the staff begins preparations to pump her stomach.

In contrast to Friday night, my Saturday is calm and peaceful. Linda and a very pregnant Katie go to a baby shower thrown by one of her old college friends. I'm left at home to do my paperwork and to wonder how I got old enough to have a daughter with her own *old* college friends.

I spend some of my alone time updating our financial projections. Daniel recently broke up with his girlfriend, so the once-delayed wedding is now completely off. I'm sure there are some disappointed people out there, but, if Daniel isn't one of them, then I guess I'm not either. As a by-product, our little family financial ship of state can sail on for a bit longer before I'll need to refuel it from my 401(k).

Marietta, Monday, October 4

Last night's cold weather snap proved that my apartment's furnace isn't working, but at least I know that now, before winter closes in. Today is also the first day of pharmacology, a course that will run for the rest of my time here and provide tools for those of us who don't expect to become surgical PAs.

Dr. Waller will lecture via Internet from South Dakota, but he's here this week to kick things off in person. He's a pleasant, approachable guy and a fellow University of Maryland graduate. He gives us each a set of his lectures on CD and then assigns a two hundred–slide presentation to watch before tomorrow morning. We already have a physiology exam tomorrow, so it's going to be a late night.

The class ahead of us is also on campus today for one of its callback days between clinical rotations. Team George alumna Madeline is here, along with my big brother. Our rotations don't come until next year. For now, all we can do is listen to their stories with envy.

Stan, Jan, and I make a presentation on Chinese health practices. It's a mix of eastern medical practices and government policies, with Stan adding some local color from his time in a Buddhist monastery. Assuming the ratio of male to female births is constant around the world, there appear to be about one million unaccounted for female births in China every year.

Stan, Drew, and I walk home after class, up the Fourth Street hill and past the old mansions. It is a classic midwestern fall afternoon, and early Halloween pumpkins dot some of the front porches. Washington Elementary is just letting out, and young parents are lining up to pick up their kids. Farther along, we pass the Quadranaou, where the leaves are just starting to turn.

It's noticeably colder Wednesday, and my car is coated by the first frost of the season. After a full day of lectures, we have another flag football game. Team Dartos falls in triple overtime to a team of athletes from some of Marietta's intercollegiate teams. Fortunately not too many of my classmates are limping as they leave the field in search of some postgame beer.

I have to beg off on the festivities. My furnace has been fixed, but Kathy and RaeAnn have a broken one, and they've asked me to come take a look at it. It seems to be in good working order but never gets warm and then shuts off after a minute or two. We search for the gas meter, where I find the supply valve locked in the "off" position. I ask if they've opened an account with the gas company, and the question elicits a puzzled stare. Kathy says that she will take care of it in the morning and thanks me for being their substitute father away from home.

We're learning about mechanisms of the liver this morning in pharmacology. It's the body's main chemical plant and determines how long some drugs will stay active before being reduced to an alternate form for elimination. On the other hand, some medications are inactive when swallowed, sometimes just to survive the acid bath in the stomach, and the liver determines how long their activation will take. Grapefruit juice can cause some interesting effects because it destroys one of the liver's many processing enzymes. Until the enzyme can be replaced, a chemotherapy drug may stay active longer than usual, but a cholesterol medication probably won't work at all.

We've been banging reflex hammers on each other's knees this afternoon. At the moment, I'm Jan's guinea pig for a test that involves her holding the base of a vibrating tuning fork against a bone in my foot to see if I can feel the vibration. I can't, and Miranda, our instructor, comes over to see what's going on.

"Do you have diabetes?" she asks.

"No, not that I know of," I answer, somewhat nervously. "Let's try this again."

I still can't feel a vibration. I had a physical before school started, but I'm concerned anyway. Like many medical students, I already worry that I have every disease we've been talking about. Failing such a simple test only makes my paranoia that much worse. Then I begin to wonder if Jan damped out the vibrations somehow, maybe by accidentally brushing against the tines of the tuning fork. I carefully repeat the test on myself, and I can feel it this time. No diabetes...at least for now.

We say good-bye to Dr. Waller on Friday. From now on, he'll be a two-dimensional image on the monitor in our distance-learning room. I'm in Columbus by dinner, sitting with Linda on a window ledge in the Cap City Diner's bar. We're sipping wine and waiting for a table. It's good to be home.

Marietta, Monday, October 11

We're dressed in shorts and T-shirts again this morning, this time waiting our turn to be tested on neurological-examination skills. While we wait, I tell the others about our squad's word-of-the-night game. Later Drew reports that he played the game today during his test, using the words "davenport," "shenanigans," and "panache." As far as he could tell, no faculty members picked up on it.

I know that I haven't yet mastered all the skills we've been taught so far, but sometimes I think I could fake them well enough to play a PA on television. I get that chance on Thursday; the college's media department is making a video for physicians who might want to be clinical preceptors for PA students. The video will eventually have a voice-over, so we're just going through the motions involved with various clinical tasks.

It's more than a little ironic, but my first role is to wear my white coat and look into another student's eyes with my professional-looking ophthalmoscope. Fortunately the audience won't know that, as usual, I can't see anything useful.

While I do get one chance to play a student, most of the time I'm cast as the patient, complete with hospital gown. That's just great! I guess I'm the only one here old enough to look the part. OK then, I'll be a method actor. What's my motivation for this scene? Should I clutch my chest and pretend to be having a heart attack? Should I complain loudly about an erection that has lasted more than four hours?

While I do my thing, my classmates play out their roles as health-care providers. I'm in a bed, and they peer down at me, feigning concern. Should

I demand a laxative? Act demented? They listen to my heart (it must still be ticking!) and write heaven knows what on their clipboards. Am I a goner? Do they want me to sign a do-not-resuscitate order?

After our fleeting acting careers, I catch a quick dinner and take tonight's research design exam. Afterward many of us go to Kim's to watch the television show *ER* as a group. While her hyperactive cats, Sass and Frass, race around the room, we settle in and become professional TV critics.

Linda often tells me that watching a medical show together isn't much fun for her. I find it hard not to critique what would and wouldn't be done in an emergency room, and she would rather not have me ruin the show. Tonight I find that watching TV with a roomful of PA students takes media criticism to an entirely new level. Absolutely no melodramatic conversation, bizarre diagnosis, or improbable treatment gets by without hoots of derision.

A light rain is falling Friday as Jan and I get together after a lecture. She would like some help with her math skills, and I've asked her, a graduate athletic trainer, to help me with my musculoskeletal physical-examination techniques. I help her with some of the ratios used in drug dosage calculations, and she helps me with spine and lower-limb tests. Slowly things start to make sense for both of us. I also learn that I have some damage in my right knee and very tight hamstrings. Hey! There are more than a few miles on these babies.

After class, I find Linda already at the apartment. She's in town for tomorrow's White Coat Ceremony that signifies the start of our transition from the classroom to the clinic. Skyler hangs out on the bed while Linda and I have dinner with Stan and his sister, who is also here for the festivities.

Our class, accompanied by many family members wielding cameras, assembles Saturday morning in the Great Room of Andrews Hall. While the college president looks on from the audience, faculty members help us slip on white coats, each emblazoned with the school patch that Jan sewed on for many of us. The short, waist-length coats mark us as medical students. After we graduate, we'll move on to the knee-length coats of clinicians.

The past president of the American Academy of Physician Assistants speaks, as does the president of the class just ahead of us. The faculty awards one full scholarship in each class, and ours aptly is being given to Melissa. She's one of the nicest people I've ever met, and she plans to work in Appalachia after graduation. Then, standing as a group, we recite the physician assistant oath.

I pledge to perform the following duties with honesty and dedication:

> I will hold as my primary responsibility the health, safety, welfare and dignity of all human beings.

I will uphold the tenets of patient autonomy, beneficence, nonmaleficence and justice.

I will recognize and promote the value of diversity.

I will treat equally all persons who seek my care.

I will hold in confidence the information shared in the course of practicing medicine.

I will assess my personal capabilities and limitations, striving always to improve my medical practice.

I will actively seek to expand my knowledge and skills, keeping abreast of advances in medicine.

I will work with other members of the health-care team to provide compassionate and effective care of patients.

I will use my knowledge and experience to contribute to an improved community.

I will respect my professional relationship with the physician.

I will share and expand knowledge within the profession.

These duties are pledged with sincerity and upon my honor.

Picture taking begins in earnest once the ceremony ends, and the guests start milling around. Some of the parents stop by to talk, often to ask me what it's like being back in school at my age. One father tells me that he has always wanted to be a teacher, and, if I can go back to school, then maybe he could too. I'm getting used to my presence here being something more than a personal adventure. If it also provides others with a glimpse of their own possibilities, then I'm happy to share what I can.

It's sunny and cool Sunday morning when we awake in what Linda calls our "getaway apartment." I make breakfast, and Skyler joins in, eating out of a spare dog bowl we keep here for his visits. Later we leave him behind, take a picnic basket with us to the boat landing, and board the excursion stern-wheeler *Valley Gem*.

The *Valley Gem* motors up the Muskingum River for a few miles and then retraces its steps and enters the Ohio River. As the autumn colors reach their peak in the afternoon sun, we cruise past Marietta and head upriver. Linda and I sit on the open upper deck and enjoy our picnic lunch of sandwiches, sliced apples, crackers, cheese, and wine. Later the stern-wheeler enters a lock, raising the boat twenty-six feet to the level of the upper reaches of the Ohio. As the afternoon grows cool, we move down into the cabin for the trip back to port.

It's been a great day, and, when it's over, Linda and Skyler drive off, and I go back to my studies. School is a succession of milestones, and more are always just ahead. In the immortal words of Dr. Seuss, I have to wonder about all the places I'll go in my new short, white, medical-student coat.

CHAPTER 13

WAITING FOR NEWS

Marietta, Monday, October 18

Someone thought to save leftover cake from Saturday's reception, and Michelle added some homemade pumpkin cookies of her own. Now we have carbs, calories, and camaraderie to add to the wall-to-wall lectures. As the week rolls by, the cold, rainy weather and long days of sitting begin to take their toll. My mind wanders during a lecture on multiple sclerosis.

Multiple sclerosis...MS...Doesn't MS sound a lot like MD...muscular dystrophy...Mom and I used to collect donations during Mothers March Against Muscular Dystrophy. Those were cold, snowy Saturdays. We'd go door to door in the frigid wind, take the money to the main fire station to be counted by men at long tables. The room was full of cigarette smoke. You would want to close your eyes...close your eyes...That welcome cup of hot chocolate, tasty and warm, the large heater. I could sit next to it and warm my cold feet. Stomach and feet now warm, I could just close my eyes and drift off...driffft...

A nudge from Stan and my eyes pop open. I valiantly try to refocus on the slides.

I check my e-mail after dinner, before starting a review of what I more or less slept through this afternoon. There I find a message from Dad, discussing treatments he has been getting for macular degeneration. Besides my parents, friends are also starting to ask me for medical opinions. We've been warned to tread carefully here since our real medical knowledge hasn't nearly caught up with what people assume we already know.

I have permission to leave my phone on in class, but the stakes are growing as Katie's due date approaches. The phone silently vibrates during an afternoon lecture, and I dart into the hallway to take the call. It turns out to be Daniel, wondering if he should bother to open a 401(k) at his new job. Yes, Daniel, you should. It might, one day, give you new options, too. I try to sneak back into class without causing a stir, but everyone—including the instructor—looks at me for news.

Friday is a short day of class, and I use the extra time to catch up on my studies. Exams are bunched up ahead like telephone poles on a highway, so studying mostly consists of focusing on the next one ahead. For most subjects, I study from condensed outlines I build from my notes and the many PowerPoint presentations we sit through every week.

Anatomy was my challenge last summer, and this time it's pharmacology. We're continually being introduced to new drugs, each with its own indications (when it can be used), contraindications (when it shouldn't be used), mechanisms (why it works), side effects, drug-to-drug interactions, advantages, and disadvantages. That's a lot to learn.

Some classmates, like Kevin, make large tables to study from. Each drug takes up a row, with each column representing one of the drug's various properties. Others, like Drew, invent mnemonics to remember the many factoids. Tables don't play well with my fading rote memorization skills, and don't even get me started on mnemonics. I would probably remember the mnemonic and forget what it's supposed to stand for.

Instead, I've started drawing elaborate drug family trees that represent each of the classes of medications we're learning. For example, one large tree provides an overview of antibiotics, while another highlights just one class, the cephalosporins. I use a lot of color, too, showing adverse actions in red and a drug's strong points in green, for example. Drawing these trees takes time, but even the mechanical task of drawing helps me organize the material in my mind. Thus far, I've been able to recall the shape of each tree and most of its contents during our exams.

When classes end for the week, I drop Drew off on my way back to Westerville. Linda has to leave for a business trip, which has her worried that it might make her miss our grandson's birth. Katie, on the other hand, is now a week away from her due date and concerned that "nothing is happening." Saturday eventually turns out to be another non-birthday that I spend running errands. Later I watch football with our apparently disinterested dog and then leave for London and a night shift on the squad.

One of our runs tonight is well out into the rural countryside. We find a seventy-five-year-old woman lying on a couch, complaining of weakness and nausea. She arrived home from the emergency room only this morning after being treated for uncontrolled high blood pressure. She hasn't been able to hold down much in the way of food or liquid all day.

Our patient is pale and warm, with a persistent headache. Her blood pressure is fine, and we decide that she is probably dehydrated. We take her to our truck, where we give her oxygen, connect her to our heart monitor, and start IV fluids, along with a medication to treat her nausea. She gradually starts to look and feel better during our long ride to the hospital.

Marietta, Monday, October 25

It's a bright fall morning, and I zip on a light jacket for the walk to class. Between lectures on chest and lung examinations, I stop at the rental office to hand over my sixth monthly check. I'm surprised that my year in Marietta is nearly half over. My walk home in the afternoon takes me past the Quadranaou, now covered in fallen leaves. Teams of small boys practice football at the base of its mound, wearing oversized, pumpkin-colored helmets that seem especially appropriate for the season. Families watch from lawn chairs and shout encouragement.

Dr. Hogan's three hundred–question exam doesn't disappoint us on a foggy Tuesday morning, taking up every bit of the allotted two hours. We're halfway through an afternoon ethics lecture when my phone begins to vibrate. Once again, I dart out of the room, and, once again, it's just a false alarm. I'm back in my apartment after class, drawing more drug family trees when Stan calls. "What are you doing?" he asks. "Drew and I are going to the Harmar for a beer, and he was wondering what 'the old guy' was up to."

Old guy or not, it sounds like a plan.

It drizzles most of Wednesday through lectures on antihistamines, asthma medications, and nerve tracts of the spine. Thursday is sunny and cool, and, at the end of a long day of lectures, most of us gather for a Mexican dinner before our evening class.

Seren has secretly told the waiter that today is Jen's birthday, which, of course, it isn't. As we're finishing our meals, a group of waiters comes over to our long table, places a large, ornate sombrero on Jen's head, and starts singing a loud, unfamiliar song in Spanish. While Jen beams at the singers, Seren sneaks up behind her and presses a plate full of whipped cream in her face. She erupts in laughter, holding the sombrero with one hand while she clears the cream from her eyes with the other.

Marietta, Monday, November 1

I turn the page on the family calendar clipped to my fridge, and the new picture of the month, showing my kids making funny faces, starts my day off with a smile. It's a day spent learning about the ear, papering the wall with drug family trees, and trying to master the physical examination of the heart.

My uphill, afternoon walk home gets me thinking about my general physical condition. A college student's life is more physical than that of the pasty middle-aged management consultant I used to be. I walk almost everywhere these days, and I seem to be in better shape because of it. Maybe the time has come for me to try a noncontact intramural sport, if one comes along.

It's dark and rainy tonight when I get a call from Jim. He's an old client and friend who just happens to be on vacation up the road. Actually he's deer hunting; Dr. Bauer should be happy that someone is trying to thin the local herd. I invite him over for dinner and a chance to get out of the rain. We catch up on each other's lives over some Trader Joe's lamb chops and wine.

Wednesday is cold and dreary, with no news on the grandson front. My phone suddenly goes off midday Thursday in the midst of Dr. Hogan's physiology lecture. This time, it's not a drill.

"What was the call?" Dr. Hogan asks as I walk back into the room.

"My daughter is in labor and on her way to the hospital," I reply. I sit back down, pick up my pen, and wait for him to start lecturing again. He doesn't. He just keeps staring at me.

"Well," he finally asks. "Aren't you leaving?"

"It's her first baby, so it will probably take hours," I reply. "I'll leave after class."

An experienced grandfather himself, he replies, "Go home now. Be with your family. This only happens once."

Not a bad idea. I get up, bid everyone good-bye, and leave to the sounds of their good wishes.

CHAPTER 14

STUDENT GRANDPA

Westerville, Thursday, November 4

There is still no grandson on the scene when I get home, and, fortunately, Linda is back from her business trip with time to spare. As afternoon turns into evening, our son-in-law's periodic telephone updates let us know that things are going slowly at the hospital. While we wait, Linda's brother Ted calls. Their son and daughter-in-law just had a baby boy today, so now I have become a great-uncle while waiting to be a grandfather. These are uncharted waters, indeed.

Tom calls again just before five o'clock Friday morning to announce that Patrick Jacob Knostman has decided to make today his birthday. Patrick already has his father's last name, so Tom and Katie picked first and middle names that relate to our side of the family. "Patrick" is a reference to Linda's Irish heritage, while "Jacob" is the name of my father's closest cousin. We're both honored.

We're at the hospital—by invitation—mid-afternoon to see Katie, Tom, and Patrick, who clearly is a handsome dude. The rest of the weekend is a blur as we help the new family prepare to come home. Being a college student goes on the back burner, and there's no time—or inclination—to study. Just time to enjoy and wonder what this new life will be like.

The birth of your child is the beginning of a life-changing family voyage. The birth of your grandchild, on the other hand, is more like watching the launch of a rocket carrying your genetic heritage into an unknowable future. You're there as it lifts off and starts its slow climb into the bright sky atop a column of fire. You can watch it for a while, but, as it picks up speed and shrinks in the distance, you can't follow it for long. For that young voyager, and on a day not so very distant, you'll only be a memory.

Godspeed, young Patrick Jacob. You come from a hardy and loving stock. May you have a long and very happy ride.

Marietta, Monday, November 8

Being a new grandfather makes this week's transition from home to school even more of a culture shock than usual. No one else in class has children—let alone grandchildren—so bringing in pictures of Patrick probably emphasizes my age. No matter, I'm just happy to have a healthy grandson. I am, on the other hand, not so happy to be taking a repeat pharmacology test without having studied over the weekend. Fortunately my original grade was good enough to stand.

Team Dartos again takes the field after class Wednesday, this time against a group of varsity baseball players. Unlike us, they're not a coed team and clearly take their sports seriously. It's humorous watching them act like they're in the Super Bowl, rather than just playing intramural flag football at a small college in southeastern Ohio. I especially enjoy listening to our women snicker at their macho, young-guy behavior. Of course, we do get crushed, but we keep our sense of humor in the process.

The weather finally takes the big turn from early to late autumn, and Thursday finds the trees bare at last in a cold rain. After dinner, I find it especially difficult to drag myself back for our research design class. We PA students sit together at the back of the hall, sometimes ignoring the lecture in favor of quietly studying for tomorrow's physiology quiz.

Friday is a short day of lectures because the class is leaving early for this weekend's state PA conference in Columbus. Linda and I have invited everyone to our house, and all twenty-one show up, along with Jan's husband and Drew's fiancée. Laughter fills the house. I half expect to see our children among the guests; this collision of my two worlds reminds me most of one of their graduation parties.

I run into Fred, my old medic-school friend, at Saturday's conference. We would be sitting together and talking if we were here on our own. Instead, we're more like intergenerational coconspirators, speaking only briefly and spending most of the time with our own classmates.

Marietta, Monday, November 15

Dr. Hogan lectures on kidney function today. I find it interesting, especially how each of the kidney's millions of filtering elements work by ingeniously taking advantage of differences in sodium concentration along its length.

After class, I run into my landlord outside of my apartment. He's an interesting guy and something of an entrepreneur. It's obvious that he really admires this old building. He has tried to rehabilitate it to twenty-first-century standards without removing too many of its charming old features. I tell him how much I enjoy the skylights in my apartment, but that I'm puzzled about how they work, given that I live on the ground floor.

He takes me upstairs and shows me a most unusual room. It's located between two of the upstairs apartments and directly above mine. In its ceiling is an exterior skylight. Two of the room's walls have translucent windows so that the apartments on either side can get some of the light. The floor of this room, which is the ceiling of my apartment, also has translucent panels that serve as my two skylights.

Unfortunately the exterior skylight was painted over many years ago, except for one small patch, greatly cutting down the amount of light coming in. Someday my landlord hopes to scrape off the rest of the paint, but, judging from what he has left to do just to get the rest of the building ready to rent, I'll probably be long gone.

My skylight lights up especially brightly just before sundown and I have always wondered why. Now I know. Light from the setting sun shines through the front window of one of the upstairs apartments. When the angle is just right, those rays shine into the skylight room through the translucent window in the wall and fall on its floor, briefly illuminating my skylights.

Tuesday starts with a lecture on cystic fibrosis, followed by a continuation of Dr. Hogan's tour of the kidneys. There isn't enough time left to go home for lunch, so Drew, Stan, and I return to the newly reopened Brownie's Market for pepperoni rolls. It's good to see Brownie's back in business, especially after all the post-flood speculation about its future. Most of the stores that were flooded have also reopened.

Dr. Waller starts Wednesday morning with a televised lecture, and, later, we learn how to perform a proper abdominal exam. After sitting all morning, it's a nice change of pace to be doing something with our hands, eyes, and ears. We slip into our gym clothes to practice on each other. This part of the exam involves listening with our stethoscopes and then looking at the abdomen under tangential lighting. Last, there is light and then deep palpation, or pressing with our hands, to see if there is pain in any of the quadrants surrounding the navel.

After nearly six months of eating at various places around town, Drew, Stan, and I are ready to try something new. Kevin has recommended an off-the-beaten-track diner that he says has fantastic dollar hamburgers. It's in a small village about thirty minutes away. We shoehorn ourselves into Drew's small car and, accompanied by his choice of rap music, drive upstream along the Muskingum River to Lowell.

We find the diner in the growing darkness. It's a nondescript, one-story brick building near the town's crossroads. We walk in a light drizzle past motorcycles and pickups to the front door, behind which we find a dark, smoky bar that time has forgotten. On its walls are faded collections of memorabilia and beer ads from another era. The other customers fall silent and turn to see who just walked in. Seeing that we're not regulars, they turn back to each other and pick up their conversations.

An older man—probably about my age, but looking like he has been ridden a little harder—comes over. Judging from his posture, he would appear to be the owner. "What'll you have?" he asks gruffly.

Stan offers, "I hear you have dollar hamburgers here."

"We don't have no *dollar* hamburgers here," the owner growls. "We have *ninety-five-cent* hamburgers and *dollar* cheeseburgers."

"I'll have two cheeseburgers. And, ah, you also have dollar beer?" Drew adds meekly.

"*Dollar* beer?" the man sputters. "We don't have no *dollar* beer! Our beer is *ninety-five cents*! What are *you guys* doing anyway? Trying to keep track of my prices or something?"

We gently place our orders, and the cook, who looks like she might be the owner's daughter, makes our food. After studying all day, we enjoy the adventure, inexpensive food, and unusual atmosphere. And they do have great hamburgers.

Thursday starts with another of Dr. Hogan's long tests, followed by a lecture on insurance and reimbursement. I come away with the feeling that the situation is even more complicated and inefficient than it looks from a patient's perspective.

We have our CPR training in the afternoon. Since I already have a CPR card, I'm asked to help out at the infant resuscitation station. I enjoy the chance to teach a little. Kathy comes over for her run-through, shouting, "Baby, baby! Wake up! Wake up!" as she tries to arouse the baby mannequin by beating it vigorously on the chest.

"Whoa!" I chuckle. "A little shake and shout is fine, but that's more like child abuse!" Kathy and the group around her join in the laughter, and then we review the procedure together.

Friday is the last day of classes before the Thanksgiving break. After Dr. Hogan's early morning lecture, we're free until it's our turn to be examiners and patients for the abdominal physical-examination test. We've juggled the schedule so that those with early flights home can be tested first. By mid-afternoon, the last ones are ready to shove off.

I pick up Stan, and we cross the river to get Kathy and RaeAnn. Stan doesn't bring home much volume-wise, but his bag is heavy with textbooks. RaeAnn and Kathy travel considerably larger. RaeAnn, in particular, travels like a movie star. I tease her that she should be referred to by just her first name, like Cher, so she has become "*the* RaeAnn." The three of them spend the night with us before catching early-morning flights.

Our break is brief, and I'm surprised at how quickly I can get used to not studying. Part of the week is taken up by appointments that would be difficult to arrange during school, but there also are opportunities for family events and seeing old friends.

Thanksgiving falls on Katie's birthday this year, and the combined celebration attracts our family, as well as our friends, the Siegels. It's also the first of what I hope are many happy family celebrations for baby Patrick. Sitting at the dining room table, I can remember a continuum of cheerful people at past family Thanksgivings. We old folks are now badly outnumbered, so we finally give up the grown-up table to the younger generation.

Soon enough, our brief break is over. I pick up Stan, RaeAnn, and Kathy at the airport and listen to their stories on the way back to school. While there is some reluctance to go back to the grind, there are just a few weeks left before our much longer Christmas break.

I move back into the apartment, kick up the heat, water the bonsai, and turn on my computer. The first e-mail I get is from the college, announcing the death of the undergraduate student-council president. He died in an automobile accident back east this morning, on his way home from celebrating his twenty-first birthday. I didn't know him but feel badly for all the sweet years that he'll miss out on.

CHAPTER 15

RITES OF PASSAGE

Marietta, Monday, November 29

I finally broke down and bought a small coffeemaker over the break. I bring its first product to class this morning in a travel mug that looks tiny next to Dr. Hogan's forty-four-ounce monster.

We have a one-on-one history-taking session this evening with several strangers who have volunteered for the occasion. My patient has had a traumatic life, having been injured in two auto accidents and also struck once while riding a bike. Just cataloging his various injuries takes up most of our allotted time.

With another pharmacology test on the horizon, Drew has made up some more elaborate mnemonics. He shares a few by e-mail:

Ok Barry, I have one for you...well, two I guess.

A fourth generation cephalosporin is Maxipime, for max money (cost), max effect, and max [generation] number (4th).

Ok this is what I really wanted to share with you. The Aminoglycosides and the Erythromycins, all have "mycin," or something close to it, at the end. So...for aminoglycosides. SNAKS-NGT. It stands for "SNAcKS" down the "NG Tube."

For Macrolides/Erythromycins "BEDZ" These are the generic names. "B", "Biaxin" for broad spectrum and big (50s) ribosomal subunit.

I think I'll stick to my family trees.

Dr. Waller introduces tuberculosis drugs on a rainy morning. Drug-resistant strains still remain, but it's striking how routine TB treatment has become. One of today's generics might have spared the lives of my grandfather and his sister in the 1920s. And first-generation drugs saved my mother-in-law in the 1940s. We're fortunate to be living when we do. Still, there's a good chance that some future miracle will come along too late to prolong our own lives.

Medical progress can be inspiring, but medical practice clearly has a way to go. We step right into this dilemma on a cool, foggy Thursday afternoon. Today we're focused on medical-service billing, which is done by visit levels that don't necessarily map into time actually spent with the patient nor patient outcome. Billing rules also force some strange inefficiencies. For example, insurance generally pays only for the least-expensive service performed on a given day. Because of that, extra visits are often scheduled for procedures that both patient and provider would have been happy to do during the initial visit.

Students from the other graduate programs on campus are making research presentations tonight in Dr. Bauer's class. It's the first time I've heard any of the Chinese MBA students speak, other than to each other in their own language. Their English is good, and they're very conscientious about their research.

One of tonight's speakers is an athletic coach whose project is an analysis of why athletes leave college early. He explains the difference between small schools like ours and larger ones, like Ohio State. Rather than leaving to go to another school or play professional sports, athletes here generally drop out to enter a trade.

After my ego is suitably deflated by Friday's physiology test, I leave student life behind and go home, where I'm once again a husband, father, and grandfather. And a son, too; my parents are in town to visit their first great-grandchild. For the first time in decades, four generations of our family gather under one roof and take pictures of all the possible combinations of people holding Patrick.

After spending Sunday morning around the kitchen table with Mom and Dad, it's time for me to leave again. Back on campus, our case team has an afternoon appointment with Dr. Kruger, who plays the role of our latest patient. He acts out his symptoms and answers our questions with his customary good humor.

Marietta, Monday, December 6

We have a few more rites of passage to go before our Christmas break. Up to now, we have done all of our physical examinations on each other and have covered most of the body. Most of the body, that is, except for the intimate male and female parts. While light snow flurries fall outside, we're lined up and waiting to perform our first male exams. We have been preparing for this for some time, but our anxiety is palpable nevertheless. We organize ourselves into teams of three and are taken, team by team, into one of two small exam rooms to meet our volunteer patients.

We find Tim waiting with our patient. He looks to be in his mid-forties and is vaguely familiar, though I can't quite place him. The five of us fill the room, and the conversation is light. Tim shows us how to do the exam, and then, one after another, we don rubber gloves and repeat the process. Our patient gives feedback as to whether or not our technique is painful and if we are pressing on his prostate with appropriate pressure. He also has a small abnormality in a spermatic cord, so we learn what that feels like.

I don't think that I'm impersonal as I do all of this, but neither am I caught up with the patient's perspective. Mostly I'm just focused on doing things right and trying not to miss anything important. This is the same mind-set I have caught myself using as a paramedic. Maybe it's even what lets me do my job. After treating someone, I usually do move on to the patient's perspective, as in, "Boy, that must have hurt!"

Like so many of our firsts, this particular experience proves to be not as difficult, nor as embarrassing, as we might have predicted beforehand. I'm still trying to remember why the patient looks familiar when I run into Stan.

"Who *was* that guy?" I ask.

"Dude! That's Bob from the Channel 52 News Team!" Stan exclaims.

"Oh, you're right!" I reply. "Watching local TV will never be the same!"

Tuesday is one of those unusual seventy-degree December days that we sometimes get in Ohio. We know it's just a tease; there will be a long wait before weather like this becomes routine again. I leave a pathophysiology exam mentally tapped out and take a break on my front stoop with a cup of coffee. Cars slow down for the light just up the street while passengers wave and say hello from their open windows.

Winter returns Wednesday, and our day starts with a lecture on HIV and the various drugs used to combat it. During a break, one of my classmates asks for advice about her grandfather. He's always asking to see her, but she seldom does, primarily because of family squabbles that don't seem to involve her.

It feels strange to be drawn into in another family's disagreements, especially one involving people I've never met. But, hey, I'm a grandfather now myself, and I have to come down on the side of at least giving the guy a chance. It doesn't sound like their relationship can get much worse, and she might just find someone who cares about her.

Before leaving for the day, we learn that just the men will have a special class tomorrow. That's mysterious enough on its own, but even more so when we learn we're to change into hospital gowns beforehand. The class is abuzz, and wild rumors abound. One grows from a comment our instructor Tim once made about his own training: students in his class did *all* of their physical exams on each other. Is that going to happen here? We hope not.

The special class is on our mind all through the next day of lectures. Though the women aren't involved, they're curious, too, and, when they're excused for the day, they look back over their shoulders at us with puzzled expressions. Now just the eight of us are left, looking at each other and wondering what will happen next. Tim sticks his head in the doorway and tells us to meet him in the clinical room.

We stand around nervously until Tim finally announces that we're about to experience what women go through when they get pelvic exams. We've been preparing for the upcoming female exams, and this exercise apparently is designed to give us some perspective. And so, one at a time, and with a palpable sense of relief, we simply lie on the examination table and place our feet in the stirrups. We get some sense of the loss of freedom and control a woman has during a pelvic exam, along with the desire to preserve one's dignity.

We decide to keep the details of our special class a secret from our female classmates, and, of course, we'll be playing it up for all that it's worth. Our first opportunity is at tonight's group dinner at Tampico's before our evening class. The women are dying to know what happened, but no straight answers are forthcoming. Instead we limit our responses to pained expressions and cryptic comments.

"It's just too embarrassing to talk about," says one.

"I just went home and cried," says another, sniffling.

"I'm just now able to sit down again without too much pain!" exclaims a third.

As far as I know, the women still don't know what happened.

Friday starts with our last lecture from Dr. Hogan. I've come to enjoy him very much, and not just because of his special insight when Patrick was born. He's also a first-rate professor and a role model for lifelong learning, even as he stands on the threshold of retirement himself. Nevertheless his long exams can drain the life out of you. He'll still be on campus next term, so I can always drop in for a talk.

A young officer from the Ohio National Guard brings lunch in for us today, along with a presentation designed to recruit PAs for service in the guard. We've been following the Iraq War, along with the bravery of several military PAs there, so there is already some interest in joining.

While most of our instructors and all of the other students stay and listen, Tim and I retreat to his office with our box lunches. As former air force captains in our fifties, we are no longer good candidates for the guard. Relaxing over our meals, we reminisce about our respective lives in the service.

Tim started out in military intelligence, spending long hours flying and eavesdropping on electronic conversations. The grind was difficult for his family, so he got out and became an emergency medical technician. He found civilian life alien and financially difficult, so he reenlisted, working in an emergency room until a slot opened up in the air force's PA program. He retired just a few years ago to begin a new career in teaching.

After lunch, it's time for our first female exams, again with volunteer patients. I enter one of the exam rooms with Stan, Melanie, and Tim. Our patient is a former nurse, who, along with a colleague in the next room, visits all of the Ohio medical schools each year. They have dedicated themselves to making sure new health-care professionals know the right way to do these exams.

Tim performs the exam while we watch carefully. Then, one by one, it's our turn. Our patient is professional and helpful, giving us continuous feedback. The process isn't as natural as listening to someone's heart or fruitlessly searching for blood vessels with my trusty ophthalmoscope. But, like so many of our firsts, having done it once, the pressure is off.

Linda is in town for tonight's holiday party, which is being held in the classroom. Everyone has brought some food to share, and Seren has concocted a tasty, yet powerful, punch. Gloria's elderly mother seems to like both Seren and his punch. Our instructors are here, too, fortunately this time without PowerPoint presentations.

For a few hours, there's no studying, just refreshments, conversation, and laughter. At one point, Kim leaves the room, returning with a banjo and a sheepish smile. She lost a bet with Seren on the outcome of the Virginia–Miami football game, so now she has to play the banjo for us. We never learn what Seren would have done if Kim's team had won.

Between the aftereffects of Seren's punch and snow flurries muffling the traffic noise outside our window, Linda and I sleep in on Saturday morning. Skyler eventually starts lobbying for breakfast, and we reluctantly get up, have some coffee and muffins, and lounge around the apartment. With finals coming up next week, we stay in for most of the day while I study, taking a break every now and then for a walk in the snow with Skyler.

We leave for home late in the afternoon for a traditional Christmas party with friends, following each other along country roads dusted by the light snow. My stay at home is just long enough for the party and ends with Sunday morning's alarm. I dress quickly in the darkness and kiss a sleeping Linda good-bye. If I don't have to repeat any tests, I should be back by midweek.

The sun is just coming up when I return to Marietta to find Skyler's abandoned dog bowls on my kitchen floor. I put on some coffee and study until it's time to meet Drew and Stan to practice our comprehensive physical exams. We practice on each other for a few hours, with Gloria stopping by at one point to answer questions. I spend the rest of the day studying for other finals, and I'm fried by bedtime. Judging from my e-mail, others are too:

From Kevin:

I ran some stats on Dr. Hogan's old tests...I know, I know. If I would have just studied them more instead of trying to beat the system, I would do just as well...but this is how my brain thinks sometimes...so I thought it might help some of you others too:

-86% of the time, "All of the above" is the correct answer

-84% of the time "None of the above" IS NOT the correct answer

-68% of the time "A and B", "B and C", "C and D", etc...is the correct answer...

Marietta, Monday, December 13

If we aren't taking a test today, then we're getting ready for one that is just ahead. By the time evening rolls around, Drew is as burned out as I am. He stops by my place for a soda and announces that he and Jodi have decided to move their wedding up by a year. They will get married this spring and then move into an apartment in Columbus before the start of his clinical rotations.

Listening to Drew's plans brings back to mind some of the raw excitement of young adulthood. After years of uncertainty, suddenly your future starts to fall into place, even though you don't know exactly where it will lead. In our case, Linda and I got married, loaded everything we owned onto a two-wheel U-Haul trailer, and got on I-70 westbound. Untold adventures flow from such simple beginnings. I wish Drew and Jodi the best in whatever their adventures turn out to be.

It's a cold, snowy morning for Dr. Hogan's physiology final, and it appears that some of my classmates spent the night studying right where they are, wrapped in blankets for warmth. For the next three hours, most of the physiology I have learned this term is painfully sucked out of me and onto paper. I leave limp, tired, relieved, and hopeful I was able to hang on to my grade.

I relax over an early lunch at the apartment and then get ready for our physical exam final. A complete exam has many steps, and I've arranged my instruments in an order that hopefully will remind me of what to do next. I plan to do the exam in a head-to-toe order, but there is a time limit to worry about. It's also frowned upon to make your patient change positions too frequently.

My number is finally up in the afternoon, first as the patient for two other students and then as the examiner. When I finish, I realize that I've skipped a few steps; I'll find out tomorrow if it was good enough. Daylight is fading, and the snow has finally stopped when we gather at the Harmar for our post-test beer. I'm happy to be sitting here with friends who have gone through nearly six months of this with me. And I know that moments like these don't last forever.

With Stan at the Harmar.

Our first semester ended in the summer's heat, and this one is ending on a decidedly colder note. Our relatively straightforward research design final is early Wednesday morning, and, when it's over, grades from yesterday's physical-exam practical have been posted. And, just like that, we're done.

I spend the rest of the day cleaning and packing for Christmas break. It's dark and in the low teens by the time I get to Kevin's for his end-of-the-semester party. He's lived here since his undergraduate days, and his old college football jersey and helmet are nailed to one wall. Beer and snacks flow, and the room churns with animated conversations.

A Trivial Pursuit game breaks out, and we split into two large teams. For once, being old here is actually an advantage. But, when we're not looking, the other team steals some of our game pieces. We eventually lose to the cheaters, but I haven't laughed this much in a long time.

CHAPTER 16

CHRISTMAS VACATION

The time off over the holidays gives Linda and me a chance to reconnect with our extended family, and we track everyone down in all the scattered places they reside these days. We start at the Maryland farm where Linda grew up.

Her old home sits high on a hill, surrounded by fields and groves of trees. It's quiet enough on a winter night to hear grains of new snow being blown across crusts of ice. There we have the traditional Chinese takeout family dinner that caps most of our trips to the farm. My mother-in-law insists that the food is for me, but I'm pretty sure that it's for her.

We're back at home in time for our family's traditional gift exchange. All of our children come over to the house, along with our new grandson. As always, we take turns finding the next present, with the latest recipient obliged to find a gift in the pile for someone else. After the last gift is unwrapped, we videotape everyone going through their loot while dinner is readied and a mountain of torn wrapping paper disposed of. Among my gifts this year are a ski cap for walking to campus on cold mornings and a satellite radio. Besides keeping me company on the drives back and forth to Marietta, the radio dismounts and should extend my selection of music to study by.

A few days later, I fly to Florida to visit my parents and drive across the state with them to see my brother and sister-in-law. While we're sitting in their living room on a sunny afternoon looking out over the Gulf, my cell phone rings. It's Tim, calling to announce that yet another flood had struck Marietta and the start of the semester will be delayed.

What fell as rain in Marietta came down as freezing rain in Westerville, and I return north to a world in which even the smallest twig sparkles in the sun like a string of diamonds.

CHAPTER 17

PIGS' FEET

Port Columbus International Airport, Sunday, January 9

Stan limps through airport security with a smile. Apparently the limp is from a vacation snowboarding accident, but you could throw your back out just hefting one of his bags. He brought his snowboarding gear back with him, too, just in case.

We make a quick pass through Marietta to assess the latest flood damage. The rivers peaked only eighteen inches below September's disastrous levels. Water still stands in the fields along the river road and against building foundations in the low-lying sections of town. Unlike September, when there was no warning, Marietta was well prepared this time. Semis lined up downtown and were quickly loaded with merchandise and equipment for evacuation. Even drywall installed after the fall flood had been screwed into place for rapid removal. Thanks to this kind of planning, the townspeople expect life to get back to normal very soon.

The river level continues to fall on Monday, which is a study day for us since classes don't start until tomorrow. Soon I have coffee brewing, and a frozen English muffin is being converted into breakfast by my trusty microwave. The new satellite radio floods the apartment with new age music while I probe the mysteries of our latest batch of new drugs to learn.

A salvo of e-mail instructions make it clear that our training will be more applied this term. Lectures will continue, but we'll also be learning hands-on skills, as well as working with patients more. There will also be guest speakers from various medical specialties, and we're supposed to be dressed business casual at all times in case a guest speaker pops in unannounced.

Before classes start on a rainy Tuesday morning, we take a few minutes to get caught up on each other's lives. I'm no longer the only one here not in his or her twenties; today is Hannah's thirtieth birthday. An honorary class member left town and isn't coming back; Seren's dog Duke was hit by a car and is staying in Florida to recover. Fortunately, aside from Duke and Stan, no one else was injured over the break. My classmate with the previously shunned grandfather took a chance and had a good visit with him. I can only imagine how elated her grandfather must feel.

Today we have our first casting lab around the benches in the clinical room. Next to each bench is a white bucket of warm water, along with trauma scissors, a supply of thick gauze, and rolls of fiberglass and plaster casting material. We're taught to put a sock-like garment over the affected limb and then layers of padded gauze. Rolls of the casting material are put in the warm water, allowed to soak for a few moments, and then carefully squeezed out. Finally the casting material is unrolled over the padding in an overlapping spiral pattern.

We take turns putting casts on each other. Soon I have a cast on my forearm, another on my leg, and I've similarly decorated Drew. At first we're led to believe that we have to keep the casts on overnight so that we can experience it from the patient's perspective. Fortunately I'm saved from limping home when we're given vibrating saws to remove the casts.

The emphasis on practical skills continues Wednesday when Miranda leads us through our first suturing lab. A blue plastic pad is placed in front of each of us, along with a pair of scissors, needle driver, and packets of sutures. Miranda then comes around the room with a plastic tub and plops a raw pig's foot down on each pad.

She demonstrates techniques for suturing different types of wounds. I try to copy her technique with my pig's foot. At first, my biggest enemies are my own clumsy fingers, but suturing becomes easier with time. After deciding on the technique and material to use, the knotting process itself is rapid. The closest experience I've had up to now is probably needlepoint. I can picture suturing like this someday in an emergency room.

We get yet another flood warning by e-mail this evening: my regular parking lot will be closed tomorrow, just in case. It's only a minor inconvenience for us, but this must be getting very old for the townspeople. Fortunately everything is still dry in the morning, which starts with lectures and a pharmacology test, followed by an afternoon workshop on electrocardiogram interpretation.

This having been a test day, I'm summoned to the Harmar for our post-test ritual. I find Stan and Drew already at a table and smiling. There's a mini-pitcher of beer in front of each of them and a bottle of Killian's next to my empty chair.

Drew is busy planning his wedding, and all three of us are looking forward to the start of clinical rotations this summer. It's a natural time to focus on the future, but I'm not yet ready to put this part of the adventure behind me. I'm enjoying the chance to reexperience college life, and tonight I try to explain how lucky I feel. And, if my life is any indication, just how different the rest of their lives will be. I'm not sure that I get my message across.

Stan hasn't been able to start his truck for the past few days, and, with the rivers threatening yet again, it would be a good idea to move it now. The sun is low when we reach the stranded truck, which is now mired in the muddy lot behind his house. Stan and Drew prepare to push the truck while I, the designated geezer, steer. We couldn't jump-start it yesterday but decide to give it one last try. Though we hold out little hope, the truck coughs, sputters, and finally starts. Stan drives it to higher ground.

We have another suturing lab on a cold, rainy Friday. This time Miranda passes out bananas instead of pigs' feet. We practice the very small stitches, running from side to side inside the skin, that are used in plastic surgery.

I'm back in Westerville by the end of the day. Tom and Katie have gone out for a rare dinner alone, so Linda and I are babysitting Patrick, relaxing on the couch and taking turns holding our grandson. I'm just happy that he's not berating me for cooing, like he did in my dream.

Marietta, Tuesday, January 18

We have a national holiday off for once, Martin Luther King Day, so the school week starts on a chilly Tuesday. I'm catching up on some reading after dinner when I hear a familiar tap at the door. It's Stan, stopping by to watch *Iron Chef America*. He's a huge Bobby Flay fan, and, over a beer, he talks about perhaps becoming a chef himself one day. His father ran a restaurant, and maybe it's in his blood, too.

Three inches of snow fall overnight, and several area schools are closed, but we aren't one of them. After a day of lectures, Gloria tells us more about the final semester on campus. Besides lectures, case studies, and skill labs, we'll also be seeing actual patients in controlled settings. We'll each get a nursing-home resident to follow and also work some shifts in a local emergency room.

It's dark and cold after dinner, but I need some exercise, so I bundle up for a walk around my neighborhood. Things are happening at the

Quadranaou, the park where, in earlier seasons, I found a vegetable stand and, later, a children's football practice. Tonight, kids are sledding in the powdery snow. It's just a short run down the gentle hill, and the action is punctuated by shouts and laughter. I watch for a few minutes, suspecting that whoever built this ancient mound would be happy to know that laughing children still play nearby.

A few blocks from home, I see a woman chasing a small dog that suddenly darts across the street towards me. She shouts for me to catch it, but I turn out to be just another part of its game. The dog veers playfully past my feeble attempts at capture. It spies two little girls farther down the sidewalk, zooms over to them, and sits down, tail wagging expectantly. The owner takes this opportunity to cross the street and grab her dog. We talk briefly, and then she walks back to her house, where her young son will be happy to learn that leaving the front gate open didn't have more serious consequences.

I'm not sure how, but even after Thursday's lecture on the pros and cons of prescribing diarrhea medications, I'm still able to eat an everything bagel with peanut butter for my mid-morning snack. The rest of the day involves signing up for our first ER shifts and listening to a lecture on the history of the PA profession.

The first physician assistant students, a class of four at Duke University, were going to school about the time I graduated from college. Thinking about that makes me wonder just how often serendipity trumps precision when it comes to picking a career.

When I was in grade school, students took something called the Kuder Preference Test. If it still exists, I suspect that it has been computerized by now. Back then, though, we were each given a straight pin and told to poke holes in an answer card. Each hole corresponded to which of three tasks I'd rather be doing. Would I rather clean a closet, catalog books on a shelf, or build a birdhouse? Count all the nails in a jar, convince someone to buy a pair of pants, or read a book?

After you ran through a large number of these choices, your unique set of poked holes was analyzed, and a report was generated. I must have picked counting nails, because my report said that I liked mathematical tasks the best. The analysis went on to suggest that I become an insurance actuary, one of the few math-oriented jobs available at the time.

Apologies to the insurance actuaries out there, but that didn't sound like the job for me. Instead I became an engineer. A few years later, I blundered into computers at work, found them interesting, and went back to school for a computer science degree. Now I'm back in school yet again and once more preparing for a career that didn't exist when I took that long-ago preference test. If my life is any indication, finding your career path can be a mysterious journey.

Speaking of journeys, tonight I'm tracking the progress of Linda's flight to Florida. She's on her way to visit her best friend Signe and her husband, Tom. Wherever they are on Sunday mornings, Linda and Signe call each other at exactly nine o'clock. Former neighbors, they joke that they may move in together as old women, should anything happen to Tom and me.

Leaving for Florida about now sounds like a good idea. It's fourteen degrees here by morning, and yet another inch of snow has fallen. We have our first guest lecturer today, Dr. Roger Anderson, a local physician who was involved in AIDS diagnosis and treatment early on. An excellent speaker, he's also the director of the emergency department here at Selby Hospital. We'll get a chance to work with him when our ER shifts start in a few weeks.

The school week ends, and soon I'm driving back to Columbus on snow-covered roads. A few hours later, I'm sitting in PF Chang's with my sons, Gary and Daniel, where we're celebrating Daniel's new job as a newspaper reporter. Somehow we end up talking about what life was like for them growing up and which of our family's traditions they would like to continue with their own children.

Gary jokingly says that he would continue the cleaning mornings, which he describes as "ripping the blankets off your kid to start the day." Daniel adds, "Then you shove a bottle of Windex in his face and tell him to start cleaning!" After the roar of laughter subsides, I remind them that eleven o'clock barely qualified as morning.

The boys talk about the dread they felt coming down the stairs on summer mornings with their sister Katie. They would look for the note Linda would write before we left for work. It was always signed, "Love, Mom" and often had little smiley hearts on it, but what the kids were most interested in was what their lone job of the day would be. Apparently their little hearts would sink if it turned out to be "clean the garage."

The boys and I say our good-byes after dinner. I spend the rest of the chilly evening at home watching TV while Skyler lies on the couch next to me. He gets up every so often to go out and roll in the new snow. Linda's e-mail tonight comes from a much different world:

We're in paradise here. The sky is blue and the water is smooth. So smooth that I can see what's in it. Off Signe's dock this morning, I saw a 6-7' alligator floating in the middle of the canal, plus two very elongated fish about 18" long that turned out to be long-nosed gar.

The palm fronds are swaying and the flowers are blooming. So nice!

I stop at Tom and Katie's Saturday on my way to ride on the squad. Patrick is sleeping, but I gather that this is not a common occurrence. After listening to their tales of sleepless nights with a colicky baby, I decide it's probably easier to be back in college and taking 9-1-1 runs in the middle of the night than to be the parent of a newborn again.

It's cold tonight at the station and far nicer to be socializing inside. It's a 2 Unit shift, so I'm riding with Carla, Jimmy, Pint, and Steve. As is their custom, the men on this shift spend the evening teasing each other, mostly in good-natured ways. I stay up late talking to Carla and, around midnight, bed down in a different place for the third night in a row. The other men are already asleep, so I have to use foam earplugs to block out the sounds of their snoring. I should have remembered just how much of an advantage it is to be the first man to go to bed.

We get our share of runs out into the cold darkness. One is to a nearby convenience store, where we find a sixty-six-year-old woman lying in the snow. Several police officers are hovering over her. She complains that a male companion pushed her to the ground, and now her right leg hurts. Fortunately she's dressed in several layers of clothing that padded her fall and kept her warm. She says she has not experienced any head or neck pain, loss of consciousness, or other injuries.

Our patient is very talkative, telling us that she's had two heart attacks, but she doesn't take any medications. Although she is concerned that she can't pay for treatment, she finally agrees to go to the hospital. We carefully put her on a backboard, strap her down, and pad her right leg in a position of comfort, braced with rolled-up towels. She never does identify who did this to her.

After another short sliver of sleep, we're called out to a truck stop on the interstate. Our patient this time is a female trucker who holds an ice bag to her left forearm. She slipped on the ice getting out of her truck and tried to catch herself with her hand.

Besides her forearm, nothing else appears injured. She can't move her left hand, suggesting a possible fracture. She does have a history of heart surgery but has no complaints of chest pain, difficulty breathing, or dizziness. We walk her to our ambulance, check her with our heart monitor, splint the arm, start an IV, give her a pain medication, and take her to the hospital.

My cell phone alarm goes off at 5:50 a.m., and I tiptoe out of the bunk room without waking the sleeping lumps around me. It's just above zero outside and still dark. My day-shift replacement has already arrived, so I can start an unusually slow trip over slick roads in a totally white world back to Marietta. I'm thirsty, but the water bottle I left in the car has frozen. I put it on the dashboard vent and, every few miles, manage to thaw a small sip.

I find that my kitchen in Marietta is only slightly warmer than the parking lot outside. It's a Sunday, so I'm on my own as far as fixing the problem. I move my gear inside and start exploring. All the registers in the apartment are blowing warm air except for the one in the kitchen. The air coming out there is so cold that the register might as well be connected directly to the outside. I get my flashlight, remove the register, lie on the floor, and peer down into the deep, cold crawl space.

Rather than using traditional, stiff, metal heating ducts, my newly remodeled apartment has flexible tubing running from the furnace to each of the registers. Peering into the crawl space, I see the ductwork as a giant, silver octopus with limbs made from what looks like clothes-dryer vent hose. The tube running to my kitchen's register has fallen off. It now lies at the bottom of the crawlspace, just out of reach. It's blowing hot air into the crawl space and displacing very cold air up into my world.

I fashion a tool out of a coat hanger, snag the tube, and force it back onto the register. Slowly the apartment starts to warm up, and soon I can take a hot shower, shave, and change out of my rumpled uniform. The world is a decidedly better place once I'm in clean clothes, sitting in a warm apartment with a hot cup of coffee and a toasted bagel.

Snow has started falling again, and it's a perfect day to stay in and study. We have a pharmacology test coming up this week, so I'm making new drug family trees and taping them up on the walls. Most of today's e-mail comes from classmates who are studying, too. Drew is probably making up more mnemonics in his apartment. Stan is likely in a commandeered classroom, writing lists of drugs and their side effects on a large whiteboard. And the usual group is probably in the small conference room, studying together as always.

Regardless of where we are today or how we're studying, e-mails are also being exchanged with Dr. Waller, who is nice enough to answer our questions quickly from half a continent away on a cold Sunday afternoon.

CHAPTER 18

BONNIE

Marietta, Monday, January 24

If there were such a thing as the dog days of winter, we would be there now. Meager slices of daylight flash by while we're in class, and the long evenings are spent studying, with occasional breaks to peer out into the blackness from behind frost-covered windows. Lecture topics for the week include infectious diseases and cardiology, but, no matter what else we're covering, pharmacology is always with us.

It can be hard starting the day early in the cold midwinter darkness, and sometimes it's all I can do to keep my eyes open in class. Classmates do doze on occasion, until their neighbors give them gentle, inconspicuous shoves. Penny is our program's administrative assistant, and many of us wander past her desk during breaks, taking some of the chocolate she keeps there for us. God bless Penny, especially on winter afternoons.

I review my answers to our latest computerized exam before pushing the "submit" button. The faculty encourages us not to change our answers if we're unsure because, supposedly, something deep within tells us which answer to pick, and our first choice is often the right one. I'm not sure that I agree, but with countless bits of new information being pumped into my aging brain every day, who really knows how I come up with the answers that I do? Maybe a trust-the-force philosophy does make sense.

It's in the single digits Thursday, and our last class of the day is an injection lab. This plays strongly into old fears some have about needles. One young woman tells me that she's afraid to stick anyone, and I offer her my arm to practice on. She works up the courage, but not the confidence, coming at me with a quivering syringe.

I wonder if part of the problem is that she's afraid she'll be causing great pain, so I convince her to let me stick her first. After all, we're using very small needles and injecting tiny amounts of saline, so there really isn't much pain involved. When she sees that the procedure is relatively painless, she goes on to give injections with more confidence. As we leave for the day, a classmate suggests that maybe I should be a teacher. Maybe I will someday.

Our week of cardiology continues on a crisp Friday morning. In an outstanding example of academic integrity, Dr. Kruger announces that he knows absolutely nothing about echocardiograms. He has, however, collected knowledge from those who do, and now he will present that to us. We appreciate his honesty, but he's researched his topic well, and within five minutes he is well over our heads.

The school week over, I collect my cargo at the apartment, and, a few hours later, I'm in London for another cold, winter night on board Medic 282. We enjoy each other's company, and the run gods are kind this time: we sleep all night without interruption.

Saturday finds Linda and me with several friends at a local bookstore for a surprise seventieth birthday party for our friend Bob. We've each bought him a book and have stationed ourselves strategically throughout the store. His family is in on all of this, so when he comes in, the surprise is complete. It's magnified when he spots his two older daughters, who've secretly flown in from California.

It's a touching event, and Bob obviously appreciates it. It's been a hard year for him and his wife, Ardy, both of whom have been fighting cancer. The present that gives them the greatest thrill is a book from their eldest daughter. Its inscription announces that they are about to become grandparents for the first time.

Speaking of grandparents, our day ends with babysitting Patrick. He's almost three months old now and smiles and laughs easily. We have a good time playing with him, and, after he goes to bed, we enjoy just sitting together on the sofa and watching TV.

Another month is coming to an end, so it's again time to revisit our financial plan. We're still OK, with some 401(k) withdrawals needed at various points ahead, until I finally go back to work. The size and timing of the withdrawals keep changing. It feels like I'm flying a small plane in a crosswind, constantly making small heading adjustments to stay on course.

Marietta, Monday, January 31

We start the week off with a lecture on cardiac birth defects. Some involve blood vessels that were supposed to close at birth but didn't. Others involve vessels that were supposed to connect to the heart in a particular order but don't—something like misplaced spark-plug wires.

Some birth defects are genetic—either inherited or the result of imperfect cell divisions. Others are caused by accidents as organs that began development in one location move past other structures on their way to final destinations. This cosmic dance of developing body parts raises the possibility for unfortunate stumbles. After a morning of this kind of talk, I wonder how any of us were born at all.

We've each been given a nursing-home resident to work with over the next few months, and, after lunch, we scatter around town to meet them. We'll be taking their medical histories, conducting physical exams, and assessing treatment plans. Though we won't be changing their treatments, they still seem like real patients to us. Actually they'll be our first patients, other than our guests during male and female physical exams last fall and the accident-prone gentleman I interviewed as part of my medical-history training.

All I know about my resident is that her name is Bonnie and she lives in a nursing home on a hill high above the river. I pull up at the home wearing nice pants, a dress shirt, a tie, and—for the first time in action—my white medical-student coat. I'm surprised to find myself a little nervous about this. I've probably seen thousands of patients in the course of twenty-odd years as a part-time 9-1-1 responder, but somehow this is different. In EMS, our interactions tend to be relatively short and problem-focused. Now I'm expected to get to know Bonnie on a much deeper level. I put my stethoscope in the coat pocket and walk in with Jeff, Aaron, and Kathy to meet our patients.

An aide takes me to Bonnie's room, where I find a smiling, solid-looking lady with gray-streaked hair sitting in a wheelchair just inside the door. Her roommate lies on the bed by the window, watching country-music videos on their shared TV. I introduce myself, and we start to talk, the music playing loudly in the background.

We start with Bonnie's personal history. She's nearly blind and unable to walk, both the result of a stroke she had a few years ago. She was born in a nearby town and worked most of her life there as a waitress and cook. She was married twice, and, more recently, lived with a boyfriend until he died. A government certificate of appreciation for his military service hangs on the wall by her bed.

Bonnie spends most of her time just listening to the television since she can only see large shadows on the screen. While her hearing has improved since the stroke, her attempts to listen to the Bible on tape have failed because she couldn't operate a tape player designed for the blind. She's a member of a local church that sends a bus to bring her to services. She's also a member of the nursing home's Red Hat Society, a national organization open to women over fifty. She laughs as she tells me how residents under fifty can also come to meetings, but they wear pink hats instead.

I finish with Bonnie's history and arrange to get together with her again in a few days for a physical exam in a more private setting. I can tell that she's happy to have had a visitor. After leaving her room, I review her medical chart at the nurse's station. It's the first chart I've ever seen, and it takes me a good hour to go through its many sections. I'm surprised to learn that Bonnie is younger than me. I'm still smiling about that when I run into Jeff and Aaron, who also find humor in the youngest nursing-home patient having been assigned to the oldest student.

It's in the upper teens Tuesday, and, during a break in a series of cardiology lectures, my attention is slowly drawn to a conversation going on behind me. Kathy and her seatmates are looking at a fashion magazine and talking about how they would like to improve their bodies. One wants a boob job, another would like to take a few inches off of her butt, and still another talks almost wistfully about liposuction.

I think the women in our class are uniformly young and good looking, so I find these comments surprising. Lines from the song "The Class of '99" come to mind: "Don't read fashion magazines / they will only make you feel ugly." I hold my tongue as long as I can, but eventually I've just got to turn around and chime in.

"Hey!" I interrupt. "You're in your mid-twenties and in your peak form! You look great just the way you are! Trust me, enjoy it!"

"*This* is my peak form?" Kathy exclaims. "What a depressing thought!"

I just shrug my shoulders and turn back around. I guess they'll just have to learn this particular life lesson on their own, like everybody else.

Every morning, I take the same walk to the same classroom building, but something is different on Wednesday. It's hard to miss the giant inflatable rat standing next to an old campus building being turned into a dormitory. Union members picket the remodeling company, holding signs around the rat's haunches. The rat, which is almost three stories high and clearly visible from our classroom, delays the start of Dr. Kruger's lecture. He and I strike up a conversation. He asks if Linda ever comes to town and then invites us to join him and his wife the next time she's here.

We start our first case studies of the term today. Case-based education is becoming a major trend in medical education. Some schools supposedly teach everything as cases, but here we have something of a hybrid. We learn normal body functions, diseases, tests, medications, and other treatments in separate courses. Case studies, along with real patients, have been added to help us pull it all together.

Our cases are getting more complex as our knowledge continues to grow. We're also being taught to consider all the possibilities for the evidence at hand, which are collectively referred to as "the differential." As in real life, the most obvious diagnosis is often the right one. The medical aphorism for that is, "When you hear hoof beats, think horses, not zebras." Still, there are so-called zebras in this world, and missing one of them can sometimes have tragic consequences. For that reason, we often have to rule out some less common, but serious, conditions.

For the case at hand, one student is supposed to interview our team's simulated patient, and I draw the short straw. Miranda, our clinical coordinator, plays the role of the patient this time. She answers my questions as if she were a pudgy seventeen-year-old girl with a skin problem, rather than the attractive woman in her mid-thirties that she is in real life. I ask questions about her health background, physical ailments, medications, family and social relationships, and the like. Afterward, I write up the information and e-mail it to the rest of the team.

A guest lecturer brightens an otherwise dreary Thursday afternoon. He tells us we shouldn't feel badly if all the information being thrown our way doesn't sink in immediately. That speaks to me as I reflect on just how much more needs to sink in before tomorrow's exam. This doesn't seem to be an age-related complaint, because everyone else I talk to also feels overwhelmed.

It's been a year since my campus interview here, and I've volunteered to help with this year's session. I review applications tonight and find myself envying the prospective students, many of whom will be starting their own adventures here soon. In just a few months, it will be time to pass the torch on to the next class—or maybe just a fried-bologna sandwich and my unused box of shelf-stable spaghetti.

It's a cold and clear Friday morning as I roll out early for this morning's test, followed by one of Dr. Kruger's continuing series of lectures on blood tests. The more I learn about blood, the more I've come to think of it as so much more than a river carrying oxygen, nutrients, and immune cells. It also carries trace substances we can use to monitor body subsystems.

For example, troponin-I spills into the blood from damaged heart muscle cells, indicating that a heart attack may be in progress. The heart, when stretched by an overload of fluid, releases the substance BNP. This signals the kidneys to excrete more, and, when they can't, we have one form of congestive heart failure. Both chemical signals, along with a great many others, can be measured and used to make clinical decisions.

In spite of our focus on pharmacology, we also learn that you can over-rely on drugs. A guest internist tells us today how he tries to wean his elderly patients from as many medications as he can, one at a time, and how they're often much better off when he's done.

The week ends with another case team meeting. One of our members, an increasingly remote young woman, is convinced that our imaginary seventeen-year-old patient is deliberately making herself fat and unattractive because her father is abusing her. She expresses this theory without any apparent trace of doubt, and the rest of us look at each other with puzzled expressions. While the theory is certainly possible, nothing we've seen so far supports it. Before scattering for the weekend, we do order a social-work consult, along with asking the patient to keep a food diary for a few days.

I'm in a different world three hours later, where the 3 Unit crew—Tommy, Scott, Matt, and Carolyn—shares leftovers from the dinner I arrived too late to join in on. Among our runs tonight is one to the home of a forty-three-year-old man, whom we find lying on a couch with his girlfriend nearby. He complains of chest pain that nothing he has tried seems to cure, including the decidedly unorthodox shot of whiskey he drank a few hours earlier.

He's anxious and warm to the touch, though he did tan at a salon earlier. His heart is racing, his lungs are clear, and our pulse oximeter shows that he's getting enough oxygen. We doubt it's a heart attack, but we take all the usual precautions, including running an EKG and starting an IV, along with giving four baby aspirin and nitroglycerin. It's just a short trip to the hospital, where they can draw his blood over the next several hours to see if there's an unusual amount of troponin floating around in it.

I'm home just after sunrise, and Skyler greets me at the door. I make some coffee and quietly pay the bills until Linda wakes up, crosses the hall to my office, and gives me a hug. We spend Saturday and part of Sunday together. Then, with several tests coming up this week, it's time to leave again.

After an afternoon of studying back in Marietta, I take a break to watch the Super Bowl. While I'm not the NFL fan I once was, the Super Bowl remains an annual milestone. I was in college (for the first time) when the first two games were played and watched them with Dad. Young upstart that I was, I pulled for the Kansas City Chiefs and Oakland Raiders to knock off the Green Bay Packers. Each briefly pulled ahead, but Dad wisely kept faith in Lombardi's Packers.

Linda and I were married the summer before the third Super Bowl, and we watched Joe Namath and the Jets beat Johnny Unitas and the Colts from our little one-bedroom apartment in Ann Arbor. We've watched all of the games together since, until this one. Now here I am, sitting in Al's old chair, watching a Super Bowl alone for the first time.

Alone, that is, until there's a knock at the door. I open it to find Stan with a smile on his face and a six-pack in his hands. I watch the rest of the game with a friend from a new era of Super Bowls.

CHAPTER 19

THE FRESHMAN SHIRT

Marietta, Monday, February 7

After being missing in action for the past few days, the giant rat returns this morning. Where it goes remains a mystery. Maybe there is a business somewhere that specializes in renting giant, ugly, inflatable rats by the day. The rat remains silent on the subject as I pass.

Later, after a day of lectures, our case team meets to discuss the results of tests on our mock patient. Her food diary shows meals laden with calories and crammed with fatty foods and sugary snacks, along with a shocking lack of fruits and vegetables. Her diet isn't helping her weight or her skin. She has also denied sexual abuse, refused a Pap smear, and a mock social-work consult shows no evidence of abuse. Our suspicious team member looks disappointed, but now we're firmly on the road to simple skin issues. We discuss what would be the best, most inexpensive medication for her acne and then scatter to study for tomorrow's pharmacology test.

I continue to feel overwhelmed. We're given a tremendous amount of new information each week, and not all of it sticks. I can't recall what we were tested on just last week. Other than studying for the next test, about all I can do is keep up with the lectures. My shelves are lined with textbooks, but, while I occasionally use them to look something up, there's no time just to explore them, and I feel badly about that.

During a study break this evening, I find an e-mail from Linda. She met a retired teacher who remembers our son in high school:

Your son Daniel is a fine young man and, in my opinion, a very skilled, professional, and hardworking journalist. You should be very proud of your parenting. He is a gentleman.

It's nice for a parent to read a note like that anytime, but especially when this parent is obsessing over an exam he won't be able to remember next week. Years from now, if anyone remembers me at all, it will probably be because I was the father of three exceptional children.

On Wednesday, we learn how to draw blood samples. Again I offer to let some classmates stick me, but, as was the case during our injection lab, each approaches my arm with a determined expression and shaky hands. It reminds me of learning to start IVs in an emergency room during EMT training. I had to start fifty of them, and, like anything else, that trail had to start somewhere.

As I was setting up for my first IV in the ER, my patient asked, "Have you done this before?" Now I'm sure that I looked out of place. I was, after all, wearing a navy-blue fire department uniform instead of scrubs like everybody else. Still, I'll bet that my clothes weren't the only clue to my newbie status.

"Oh *yes*," I answered, mentally crossing my fingers. "*Many* times." Which was true if "many" could mean two people in EMT class.

I don't think my hands were trembling that day, but they could have been. I did notice, though, that the more time I spent in the ER, the fewer the patients who asked me that question. The experience taught me a valuable lesson. With any medical procedure, you need to know what you're going to do and how you're going to do it. But there's more to it than that; no matter how nervous you may feel inside, you still have to execute with the confidence and steadiness needed to convince your patient that he or she is in good hands.

Today both classmates miss my vein on their first attempt but go on to succeed. In the process, they build confidence and also help me pay back an old debt to Pete D'Onofrio. Pete was an instructor in EMT school and the first person on whom I successfully started an IV.

After the lab, we analyze the blood we've collected. This experience is tempered considerably by having to wear our anatomy lab coats again for the first time in months. No amount of washing has taken away the smell of preservatives, nor have our summer memories faded. "Hey!" quips Seren, slipping on his coat. "There's a *finger* in my pocket!"

I peer into a microscope to do a manual blood count and see one of my lymphocytes busily gobbling up what I assume is a damaged or infected red blood cell. Later imaginary blood cells dance in front of my eyes as I go off to sleep.

Yesterday's brief thaw is over, replaced by flurries and a few inches of new snow on top of an icy base. I use a midday break to study for another test. Among the diseases I'm supposed to know this time are the four basic types of leukemia. They differ in the blood cells affected, typical patient age, and likelihood of a cure. I struggle to remember which is which.

This afternoon we have a guest lecture on tuberculosis and how its treatments have evolved over the years. Ah, progress...I start to doze off. It has to be at least eighty-five degrees in here. Someone finally opens a window, and the room begins to cool down. We finish our day with light flurries blowing into the room.

It's cold and clear Friday, and some of us are having lunch at the Third Street Deli. Stan and I are sitting with Jan, who looks worried. After some gentle prodding, she tells us that she's been having severe abdominal pain on and off for the past few days. Now she has our attention. Telling PA students about symptoms, even over lunch, is a surefire way to get a conversation going.

Stan quips, "You're newly married; you're probably just pregnant." Stan is going for one of the "horses" in this differential diagnosis.

"Oh no I'm not!"

"Well," I add. "The most serious cause of sudden abdominal pain in a woman of childbearing age is a tubal pregnancy." Not really a zebra, but not a unicorn either, and one with serious consequences. "You'd better get that ruled out."

"No," Jan replies. "It couldn't be."

"Well then," I suggest. "You could just start calling the baby 'Tubie.'"

We keep teasing Jan until she agrees to see her health-care provider. Then we let her finish her meal in peace.

We have lectures and case team meetings in the afternoon, and, a few hours later, I'm back in Columbus. Linda and I are walking out of the frosty evening and into the Cap City Diner's crowded bar. Our bartender tonight is Amy, a law student we've gotten to know from our frequent dinners here. She greets us with a smile and puts our usual drink order on the bar without uttering a word. When I ask for the tab, she smiles and says, "It's on the house tonight."

"Why?" I ask, appreciating free drinks as much as the next guy.

"You two are the only ones here who look like you're having a good time," she replies.

With that, I thank her. The end of another week apart is cause for celebration. While we wait for a table, we take our drinks, sit on a low ledge against a cold plate-glass window, and get caught up on our week apart. It's good to be home.

Our family gathers Sunday for an early Valentine's Day brunch. Everyone pitches in, and the house is full of activity. Patrick gets passed around the dining room table by his parents, uncles, and grandparents while we noisily share breakfast burritos and guacamole dip. When the crowd melts away, Linda and I exchange envelopes to open on the actual holiday. Then it's time for me to leave again.

I spend Sunday afternoon studying in Marietta and then take a break to watch the first game of the season for our class's indoor soccer team. They are the same athletes who played football on Team Dartos, and, while they have changed sports and uniforms, they certainly haven't changed their style of play.

Instead of being the unstoppable running back, Julia now is unstoppable in goal, the position she played in college. Seren, the former rugby player, again plays like he's indestructible. Kevin, the former college football player, now stands in against attacking opponents, regardless of their size. And it's not long before Jeff, the emotional former college hockey player, is angrily exchanging words with the opposition.

After the game, I stop by to check on Jan on my way home. Fortunately she doesn't have a tubal pregnancy, but she will need surgery. She's in pain, but her husband is taking good care of her. I borrow her iPod so I can record the lectures she'll miss.

Marietta, Monday, February 14

I open Linda's valentine with a smile before Dr. Kruger's morning lecture. He's a pathologist by training, so we often get heavy doses of stained tissue specimens in his presentations. If you didn't know that a particular swirl of multicolored cells was, for example, tuberculosis, you might think it was modern art. Suitably enlarged and framed, it might even look good on a living-room wall.

We have case presentations in the afternoon, with our team presenting the patient with acne and the poor diet. At one point, a faculty member pretending to be our supervising physician asks, "What do you have here?" In response, a team member makes a thirty- to sixty-second, rapid-fire presentation about the patient and what we're planning to do. We try to boil down the facts and just cover what's important, but we're still new at this and tend to say too much about some things while still managing to skip important details.

134

As each team finishes its case, the class and our instructors ask questions and make suggestions. Overall, the experience has been an eye-opener. We enjoy the exercise, which pulls together the factoids we've been learning and gives us a glimpse of our futures.

Winter calls a brief truce Tuesday for a rare spring-like day buried in the midst of February, traditionally the coldest and darkest of Ohio months. We have a class pizza lunch between lectures to plan the annual spring golf scramble. Something of a tradition, each PA class hosts the event and splits the proceeds between a local charity and our graduation party next year. Given Marietta's recent history, we pick a charity involving local flood relief.

I study after class in front of an open window for the first time in months, enjoying the warm breeze and sounds of life outside. Unfortunately Wednesday dawns dreary, rainy, and cold. And even more unfortunately, my trunk is now a shallow, cold swimming pool. I must have opened it accidentally when I put my keys on the dresser last night. Nothing was taken, but it's not just a trunk to me, it's my traveling closet. I leave for class with wet squad bedding draped throughout my apartment.

Dr. Kruger lectures on lung cancer, and the luck of the draw is at work here, too. Some cancers are treatable when caught early, while others are less so. As with many of the diseases we've covered, a patient's prognosis is heavily influenced by the results of a cosmic lottery.

Speaking of lotteries, Thursday's spin of the weather roulette wheel lands on snow flurries, with the sun coming out briefly as the school day ends. It's been an exam day, and I join Seren and Jeff on the walk to the Harmar Tavern. The comfortable scene there never seems to change. Men wearing ball caps inscribed with local business names lounge at the bar, while a few couples sit nearby, talking over drinks and snacks. Our beer and sandwiches are as good as always, and soon this most recent test joins its predecessors as just another memory.

Seren and Jeff have contact sports in common, and they are natural friends. Seren is an energetic guy from Florida, but he has family not far from here, in the Hocking Hills region of southeastern Ohio. Jeff is from Toledo and lives here in an apartment with his fiancée, Paige, who's from Baltimore. They plan on getting married after Jeff graduates and moving back to the Toledo area.

Somehow the conversation turns to Marietta history. I tell them about a marker I passed earlier, honoring the Marietta College Ambulance Corps. A companion plaque lists the corps's members, twenty of whom were killed in action. Apparently it was the first unit to fly the American flag in France during World War I. That struck a chord with me since my childhood home of Rome, New York, is where the flag first flew in battle, period.

Jeff tells me about another local historical marker just a few feet from his apartment, which has something to do with Lewis and Clark. I've been interested in Lewis and Clark ever since Dad and I retraced their expedition from St. Louis to Oregon several years ago. Now I live only a mile or so from their route from Washington, DC, to the expedition's jumping-off point in St. Louis.

I find the marker on the banks of the Ohio on my way home. It describes how the Corps of Discovery stopped "across from Marietta" on their way from Pittsburgh to St. Louis, where their journey westward into the unknown officially began. To the locals then, it might have looked like a nineteenth-century version of the pictures we've seen of astronauts smiling and waving as they board vehicles to take them to the launch pad. And maybe all that took place right over there.

On Friday, our case team is introduced to its next mock patient. She's a twenty-five-year-old customer-service representative who complains of feeling jittery, along with episodes of a racing heart. It's difficult for her to get along with her coworkers, she lacks the ability to concentrate, and she feels especially tired as of late. She's also hungry all the time, even though she's losing weight. We decide on some possible diagnoses and lay out tests we would like to order.

The weekend again starts in London, where the 2 Unit shift is a happy bunch tonight. Steve, though, grumbles loudly whenever our sleep is interrupted. I've called him my Seeing Eye dog. When he starts swearing, we've been dispatched, and I know I should get up. When he stops, I know that I'm back in the bunk room and can go back to bed.

One call tonight is for a seventy-eight-year-old woman whose family couldn't arouse her. We find her lying on her side, unconscious, breathing poorly, and with severely swollen legs. We put her on oxygen, give her a breathing treatment, start an IV, give a diuretic, and run an EKG. Gradually her breathing improves, and she becomes more alert on our ride to the hospital.

I get some sleep and come home to find Linda in bed, bracketed by a sleeping dog and cat. I half expect to see the dog wearing my pajamas one of these mornings.

Over the weekend, an e-mail arrives from a coworker of mine from twenty years ago. He's still part-time with the same company, though he's officially retired.

> For reasons I don't fully understand, I still have a badge and part time status. So I go in now and then. Just enough to remind me it is not the place I knew. Almost no one I knew is there now. Now the people who are there accept it as it is. Such is life. It's an old line, but remember: for today's kids, these will be the "good old days."

I don't know exactly what I'll be getting into with this new career of mine, but I'm happy not to be mourning the passing of an old one.

Marietta, Monday, February 21

It's cold and rainy this morning when I get up, or, to be more precise, when I try to get up. I have a fever, along with some congestion and a sore throat. Maybe my macrophages didn't eat all of the infected red blood cells after all. After some coffee and a few over-the-counter medications, I'm ready to take a shot at the day. I'm not alone in being under the weather; several chairs are empty this morning. In an interesting display of synchronicity, our first lecture of the day is on ear, nose, and throat infections.

With a guest speaker coming after lunch, I need to change into a business-casual outfit. On the spur of the moment, I decide that it's time to carry on an old tradition. I change into a very special shirt.

How can a shirt be so special? Well, I'm something of a pack rat, which probably explains why this particular shirt has hung in various closets of mine for the past forty years. In my defense, it's really not just *any* shirt; it's the one my parents bought for me the week before the start of my freshman year. It's truly a survivor; even the College Park, Maryland, store it came from is long gone.

I walk into class wearing my old, short-sleeve, blue-and-white striped freshman shirt. No one seems to notice that maybe it's a little snugger than the rest of my wardrobe. I probably weigh thirty pounds more now than I did when I was eighteen, but, happily, no buttons were harmed in the filming of today's episode.

I've perked up a bit Tuesday, and we find out the results of our mock patient's lab tests. We've successfully diagnosed an overactive thyroid in our irritable customer-service rep. This is getting to be fun.

My cold is hanging on, and I'm beat by the end of the day, but we have to come back after dinner for a guest speaker. He's from a well-known business school, and tonight he is pontificating from the front of a large auditorium on the business of medicine. I don't expect to retain much of this and start to doze, but it isn't long before his comments annoy me back into consciousness.

Our guest believes that, in the interest of economics, health-care should be rationed. To illustrate his point, he goes for cheap laughs from the overwhelmingly young audience by condemning health plans for paying for Viagra. He's making a moot point here: most health plans don't pay for Viagra. What disturbs me even more, though, is that he feels preserving your sexuality for as long as you can is somehow a frivolous eccentricity. Kind of like a fifty-eight-year-old guy wearing his freshman shirt to class, I suppose. After having four friends commit suicide in their fifties, I'm not inclined to be quite so glib about middle-age self-images.

I'm back in my apartment by half past nine, feeling rocky and ready for bed. This was to have been my first shift in the emergency room, but I call in sick. The only way they're going to see me tonight is as a patient.

I feel better in the morning, and most of the other sickly ones are also back in their places. That includes Jan, who has been out for a week after her successful surgery. She even brings in a DVD of the procedure and plays it for us before class. We watch intently—such is the level of entertainment in PA school. There is even some food to go along with Jan's movie. It's Seren's twenty-fifth birthday, and someone baked a cake.

This scene reminds me of another college birthday: Dennis Goodman's twenty-fifth back in the Dark Ages at the University of Maryland. Dennis was an army veteran and a few years older than the rest of us. We surprised him that day in the engineering honor society lounge, where someone had written "Dennis Goodman: Celebrating a Quarter Century of Progress" on the blackboard. Somehow twenty-five seemed a lot older to me then than it does now.

Our next test is only a few days away, and so, by evening, I'm back to studying and trying to fight off the stubborn bug that has been trying to get me. I turn in early, with a sense of contentment as I close my bedroom door, crawl under the heavy quilt, and turn off the light. The last sound I hear is the whir of my small humidifier.

CHAPTER 20
WHAT A STRANGE LIFE I LEAD

Marietta, Thursday, February 24

There are changes all around this morning, starting with the weather. A heavy overnight snow buried any hope for an early spring. The sound of footsteps overhead signals that my time without a neighbor is at an end. And a sign out front announces the grand opening of a tanning salon where the young wedding planners used to be. The snow tapers off a bit during afternoon classes, and I spend the evening papering my walls with notes to study for tomorrow's test.

I'm up early on Friday and feeling pretty much back to normal. I drive in for a lecture on dementia, the irony of which is not lost on my aging brain, now hopefully crammed with useful factoids for today's exam. We have a break before the test, which most of the class uses to cram some more. That doesn't work well for me, so I just relax over a newspaper and coffee at Izzy's.

I get back to the apartment at the end of the day, just as Linda and Skyler show up on my snowy back steps. We are tired from our respective weeks and happy just to stay inside and relax. Skyler joyfully races around the apartment until he gets tired and lies down next to us.

I'm staying in town this weekend to help with the new-student interviews. The applicants arrive Saturday and are interviewed in groups of three by two different teams of faculty members, current students, and recent graduates. The visitors are free to relax in the lounge between interviews, have refreshments, and talk with some of our class. It was those conversations last year that did the most to convince me to come here.

Those of us on the interview teams have considerable latitude with regard to what questions we can ask. Besides the obvious ones—like, "Why do you want to be a PA?" —part of the ritual includes asking some whimsical questions, too. These can probe an applicant's understanding of the profession, as well as problem-solving skills and the ability to think on one's feet. Classmates who took part in last weekend's interviews report that some of the applicants were fairly tightly wound, and their answers could be rocky.

"What would you do if you were already a physician assistant," asked one faculty interviewer last week, "and your supervising physician was about to do something that you thought would kill the patient?"

"I would rush over and tackle him, sir!" responded the applicant, sounding like one of the characters in the movie *Police Academy*.

Another applicant was asked which part of the human body he would choose to be and why. That's a strange question to be sure, but the interrogator was more interested in the applicant's ability to think on his feet than on any possible correct answer. The applicant blurted out that he would like to be a sperm, but then became tongue-tied trying to explain why. Several minutes into his convoluted answer—agonizing for all concerned, I'm sure— he decided that he'd rather be an ear. Good choice.

We meet several good applicants today, including a thirty-nine-year-old female firefighter/paramedic. A classmate tells me that she's concerned that she might be too old—at least until she hears about me. I track her down later and tell her, tongue in cheek, that she would be a great candidate if only she wasn't so darned young.

By the time we're finished, Linda is back from visiting her friend John, who raises horses and birds on a small farm about twenty miles up the Muskingum. He used to live farther north, on a large farm in Ohio's Amish country. We once spent a memorable, intercultural day there at a large picnic he threw for his Amish and what they would refer to as his "English" friends.

Tonight we're joining Joe Kruger, my pathology instructor, and his wife Ruth for dinner on a restored, moored stern-wheeler, the *Becky Thatcher*. It's a chance to see the non-pathology side of Joe, but apparently not the non-pathological; he turns out to be a huge horror-movie fan with an extensive video collection. Joe went to Marietta as an undergraduate, where he met Ruth, who was, in his words, "a townie." They're good-natured foils for each other's stories.

Marietta, Monday, February 28

The theme of our latest unit in pathophysiology became evident this morning. It's a virtual cruise down the digestive tract. We start with some small bowel disorders, followed by stool samples. I can hardly wait for lunch. Actually, not much affects my appetite these days, which is probably the result of riding on a squad for all these years. After you've had enough interrupted dinners, you learn to eat what you can, when you can.

I stop at the nursing home during a break in our schedule for Bonnie's physical exam. Residents in the foyer greet me with smiles and a friendly, "Hi, Doc," which only adds to my general feeling of being an imposter in a white coat. It's a common enough emotion in new situations. I once worked with a young corporate vice president who had his own imposter scenario. He dreamt that two visitors suddenly burst into his well-appointed office. One pointed at him and said, "*There* he is, officer! Take him away!"

It's been a few months since I did a complete physical, and I seem to have forgotten some of the steps. Bonnie is a willing participant, but she is wheelchair-bound, nearly blind, and her movements are limited as a result of her stroke. We keep up a running conversation while I work. Yesterday was her fifty-second birthday, but she was ill, and her party had to be postponed. I admire her positive attitude, especially given some of the unfortunate events in her life.

The sudden death of my otoscope battery signals the premature end to today's exam, and I arrange to finish it tomorrow. I mull over my rusty exam techniques on the way home in a driving rainstorm. We're getting new information thrown at us every day, and now it looks like even the skills that I thought I had already mastered are slipping away. In my case, maybe the fire hose of knowledge is being sprayed into an old sieve.

At home, I find an e-mail from RaeAnn:

> We are putting together a little fundraiser in honor of Seren. Kim and I have decided that he needs new shorts (i.e., longer ones). If any of you have played or watched the sporting events that he participates in, you would understand.
>
> His shorts are usually shorter than most of the girls playing. We are thinking of heading to the mall to see what we can find to help the poor guy out. If you would like to donate a dollar to Seren's shorts, great!!

I've seen his shorts; my dollar is on the way.

Our cruise down the digestive tract continues on a snowy Tuesday. We bid a fond adieu to the small intestine and sail on downstream into the colon and its unique set of diseases. When lectures end for the day, it's time for me to finish Bonnie's physical exam. She told me yesterday that, if she could read again, she would like it to be something religious. I stop at the county library on my way to the nursing home and check out a books-on-tape player and a religious tape.

Bonnie is her usual cheerful self, and we finish the rest of her physical in a few minutes. Then she tries out her new tape player that, unfortunately, is a lot like the one she tried before. The buttons are hard to find and difficult to press. It really is an unusual design for a product geared toward elderly, visually-impaired customers. Bonnie decides to give it a try anyway.

Snow blows across the roadway in thin strands on my way back to the apartment, where I shed my white coat and get to work analyzing Bonnie's medications. When my stomach signals dinner, I whip up some spaghetti with turkey meatballs and a salad with pine nuts. Then it's time to study until bedtime.

Still more snow falls overnight, and we pick up on our digestive tour in the morning. There's a detour after lunch, when a guest speaker discusses oral diseases, especially those that can give clues to systemic conditions. Because so many patients don't get good dental care, PAs often get involved on the fringes of dentistry.

Tonight I'm at the last indoor soccer game of the season. As the only fan present, I take pictures for players who brought their cameras along. We win 4-1 against the college's athletic coaches and finish the season undefeated. It helped a lot that Julia has been our goalie. She was first-string on her college team, and I don't think she gave up more than three goals for the season. This is the second intramural sport that I've been a spectator for, but soon I'll be leaving the sidelines to play on our new volleyball team. Hopefully it's a sport I can still play without hurting—or embarrassing—myself too much.

Stan has already started his ER shifts. After the game tonight, he sends out an e-mail epiphany:

> I came to a strange point in my life today. Early this afternoon, one of our classmates asked me "Is all of this worth it?" I told this person that "yes, it is."

> Just now—this very minute at 21:36 March 2nd—I realize that I really like being here. I have met the greatest people. I have played on a championship soccer team, a flag football team, and a second bracket walleyball team. I diagnosed acute exacerbated COPD, hypersensitivity to cardiac medication, performed incision and drainage, and have learned about a disorder called Tsu Tsugamushi (from chiggers).

What a strange life I have; this time last year was very different.

For me too, Stan. For me, too.

Another school week behind me, I drive home to spend the weekend with Linda. Sunday is the fortieth anniversary of our first date, and our friends Dottie and Ron have invited us out for brunch to celebrate. We all share details as to how we met our spouses.

When I first went to college, someone gave me some good advice: I could now be whomever I wanted, and the new people in my life would be none the wiser. One decision I did make was to seek out interesting women to sit next to in class. In those days, majoring in engineering meant you probably weren't going to see all that many women in your classes, interesting or not.

Fortunately our small honors English class was a notable exception, and I sat next to Linda the very first day. We worked on some projects together, but I was slow to ask her out. In truth, asking a girl out never was second nature to me. When we became parents, it was Linda who arranged babysitters; I never again wanted to call up a teenage girl to ask if she was free on Saturday night.

Just before the end of the term, I finally worked up the courage to ask Linda out. She denies it now, but I recall her answer as being, "I'm sorry, but I can't." Very confusing. Can't *what*? Can't go this weekend? Can't because my boyfriend won't let me? Can't because I don't date outside my species? What?

Whatever the meaning of "can't" was, the semester ended without a date. My English class the following term was huge, but no Linda. I finally called her a few weeks later, and we arranged to go out. At the last minute, our date had to be rescheduled when she called to say that a cow had kicked her mother. It sounded strange, but I chose to believe it. It was true, and the rest, as they say, is history.

CHAPTER 21
SHORT COAT IN THE ER

Marietta, Monday, March 7

National Public Radio provides another of life's flashbacks this morning. They're doing a segment on the fortieth anniversary of "Bloody Sunday, 1965," when civil-rights marchers were attacked on their way from Selma to Montgomery. I was in college at the time, so, while today may be young, it's making me feel old.

One of our morning lectures focuses on liver diseases. The liver is our main chemical plant, and some of its functions seem to be scheduled like those in a factory. Cholesterol, for example, is produced primarily at night. The liver is also one of the few organs capable of self-repair, as long as damage is confined to working cells. It's another matter when the critical support structure is involved, as in chronic alcoholism.

Our case team skips an afternoon work session in favor of preparing for a test. A steady rain falls while I study in the apartment, the drumming on the sidewalk occasionally punctuated by the barking of my new neighbor's little dog.

This isn't the first time I've been a student living below a dog. While in graduate school in Ann Arbor, Linda and I lived under neighbors who kept a noisy German shepherd. One spring afternoon, I was on our balcony grilling steak when their dog relieved himself on their balcony, causing the gaps in the boards over my head to take on an unfortunate new significance.

I had about a second to decide what was more washable, a poor graduate student or a really good-looking piece of meat. When Linda got home from work, her freshly showered husband presented her with a medium-rare steak. It wasn't our last apartment, but, until now, it was the last time we lived under anyone.

I'm up early Tuesday for what I hope will be a red-letter day: my first ER shift this evening. But first there is a regular student day to get through. Much of it is spent learning about the various forms of hepatitis. There used to be one, what we call "type A," but now there are at least five—each with its own cause, treatment, and likely outcome.

When classes end in mid-afternoon, Drew and I head out in the light snow flurries on a mission. He and Jodi are going to Florida over spring break, and he would like to go with a tan. He feels that the tanning salon in my building is too expensive, so today we're casing out some others. I'm surprised that there are so many salons in a city of this size, until I reflect on the gloomy weather of the past few months.

I drive to Selby General Hospital, a small eighty-bed facility on the edge of town, shortly before the start of my six o'clock shift. I'm ready for today's real adventure to begin. Just to be on the safe side, I actually test drove the five-minute route here yesterday. Now I walk nervously into an unfamiliar world, clad in my short white coat with its college name tag. Two nurses sit at the reception desk and eye me with curiosity. A guy in his late fifties wearing a medical-student jacket is probably not an everyday occurrence.

I introduce myself and am taken back to the physician's desk in the ER, where I'm happy to recognize the doctor in charge. He is Dr. Anderson, a frequent lecturer for our class. Liesl, a young, third-year medical student, is accompanying him tonight. Dr. Anderson immediately puts me at ease, taking me on a tour of the small ER and explaining its operations.

As each patient is given a room, a nurse will obtain a history and vital signs, and then bring the patient's chart to Dr. Anderson's desk. Liesl and I will take turns seeing each patient. When it's my turn, I'll pick up the chart, go in to assess the patient, develop a plan, and then return to Dr. Anderson with my recommendations. Other than the obvious live ammunition here tonight, it's quite a bit like what we've been doing in our case studies.

My very first ER patient ever is a seventeen-year-old young man complaining of a sore throat and ear pain. I introduce myself and start asking him questions about his complaints. I examine the glands in his throat and under his jaw. I use the otoscope to peer into his throat and also inspect his eardrums, which are inflamed with fluid trapped behind them.

Dr. Anderson listens patiently while I summarize my findings, along with a recommendation for an antibiotic. He smiles silently, visits the patient by himself, and returns, agreeing with my plan. It's a very simple case, but I'm stunned nevertheless. For the first time, I've pulled together some of the skills we've learned in all of those isolated classes and applied them to a real person. It was just a sore throat and an ear infection, but still, this experience has been gratifying.

Dr. Anderson gives me an early lesson on the role of administration in medicine. He leads me through the hospital's paperwork and has me write the prescription, patiently explaining the format. He signs the prescription, and the encounter is complete, or so I think.

A few minutes later, my first-ever patient leaves with a wave for me. "Good-bye, Doc, and thanks," he adds as he steps out into the snow.

One of the nurses smiles and asks, "Is that the first time anyone has ever called you 'Doc?'"

Some of the residents of Bonnie's nursing home have called me "Doc" because of my white coat, but this is the first time that I've actually treated anyone. "It is," I answer. "If we were on the squad, I'd have to buy you all ice cream."

Ice cream, by the way, is the standard treat an EMT buys his crew whenever he does something new. It might be your first cardiac arrest, delivery, mass-casualty incident, shooting, or patient flown to the hospital by helicopter. Or it could just be the first time you accidentally graze a curb with the truck's tires. In short, it's pretty much any time your crew senses an opportunity for you to buy them ice cream so that they can celebrate the occasion with you.

I get to know Liesl better during breaks between patients. She attends an osteopathic medical school in Kentucky, and, yes, she was named after a character in the movie *The Sound of Music*. I don't tell her that Linda and I saw that film on my nineteenth birthday.

Liesl sees a patient, and then the next one is mine. It's a woman who looks to be in her forties. She's in tears because she can't bear the thought that a lingering case of pneumonia has returned. I try to calm her, ask some questions about her symptoms, and then launch into an exam. I don't think she has pneumonia, just a common cold, but the medications that she has been taking for it are mostly the wrong ones. We change all that, and she goes happily on her way.

The ER gets busier as the evening progresses. Sometimes Dr. Anderson agrees with my assessments and plans, and sometimes he doesn't. Still, it's all good; I'm enjoying myself and learning as I go.

Like any night in any ER, most of the complaints are routine, and the constant flow of humanity can slowly dull your curiosity. For me, that comfortable rhythm ends shortly after meeting a sad-looking twelve-year-old girl with a slightly swollen cheek. I introduce myself and sit down so that we can talk with our eyes at the same level, as I've been taught.

"Have you been hit in the cheek lately?" I ask.

"No," she replies. "I woke up like this."

I look more closely at her face and note that the swelling is not very dramatic. I do see, however, that the right corner of her mouth is drooping ever so slightly, a sign that wasn't noted in the triage nurse's notes.

"Would you mind if I took a look in your mouth?" I ask. She nods OK.

I put on my gloves and begin probing her mouth for abscesses or tenderness. I don't find any. Then I go through tests of her cranial nerves. The same nerves I memorized last summer while parading around my apartment. And the same ones we tested on each other last fall. Olfactory, optic, oculomotor, trochlear, trigeminal, abducent, facial...

I discover that, not only is her lip drooping a bit, but she can't open her right eye against even very light resistance from my finger. Taken together, these clues suggest a problem with her right facial nerve. OK, but what could cause that?

Well, it could be a stroke—one of the more serious zebras in the differential diagnosis—but she's only twelve and she has no other history or obvious risk factors. A stroke would not be impossible, but it's not the most likely cause either. Bell's palsy might explain it. That's an inflammation of the facial nerve, often viral and of sudden onset. I settle on Bell's palsy as the explanation and go back to find Dr. Anderson. I'm way beyond sore throats now and wonder if I'm only just imagining the sound of ice cracking beneath my feet.

I describe the case to Dr. Anderson, who again smiles and, without saying a word, goes in to see for himself. He looks pleased when he comes back, agreeing with the diagnosis. "Nice catch," he says, again with a smile. "She's the youngest patient I've ever seen with Bell's palsy."

We give our patient some steroids and instruct her mom to follow up with their family physician in a few days. It's likely that the condition will clear up without any permanent damage, though it's not a certainty.

A light snow is falling by the time my shift ends. I got some diagnoses wrong tonight and occasionally forgot to do some of the things that we've been taught. Regardless, the past four hours have been the most motivational experience I've had since deciding to become a PA.

Drew and Stan have spent the evening studying, and now they call to suggest we do something fun. I invite them over, and soon we're laughing over a few beers and sharing our stories of the ER. We're getting a glimpse of our futures, and we like what we see. And maybe it's possible to apply some of the information that rains down on us in class after all.

The snow stops by morning, and I head off to campus for an all-Dr. Kruger day that focuses on liver and gallbladder diseases. I enjoy Joe's command of the material and his sense of humor, but six hours of listening to anyone is tough. A client once told me that his father-in-law decided to go to law school when he was in his late seventies. When asked why, he would answer, "Well, it's not because I expect to be on the Supreme Court." There were several nearby schools to choose from, and he eventually picked the one with the most comfortable chairs. Right about now, that doesn't sound like such crazy logic.

It's warmer Thursday, and, perhaps as a cosmic sign, we have a lecture on antidepressants right before a particularly tough pharmacology exam. Many of us go to lunch afterwards at the Third Street Deli. Lunchtime topics today include grousing about the exam and plans for our upcoming clinical rotations. About a third of the class plans to stay in town for their clinicals, including Stan, Jan, Aaron, Hannah, Kim, and RaeAnn. Drew, Kathy, Kevin, and I are among those who will be leaving.

My brother calls after class to announce that his eldest daughter, Stephanie, had a baby girl today. Lucy and her mom are doing fine, and now Scott is a grandfather, and I'm a great-uncle again. I think about all that happens among my scattered family while I'm here. Then I switch off the light and fall asleep on another snowy night in this little river town.

Logan, Ohio, Monday, March 14

Today is the college's community-service day, and our class will be spending it passing out food at a pantry run by Seren's grandfather in southeastern Ohio. Drew, Joanna, and I reach the outskirts of Logan with only skeleton directions to the pantry, but it's easy to follow the long, double line of cars waiting patiently for it to open. The regular volunteers greet us, and we're quickly assigned to our stations.

Once the pantry opens, a steady stream of cars flows through all morning long. As each car stops, the driver shows us a coupon indicating the types and quantities of food he has been authorized. Some also pick up orders for neighbors who can't get out on their own. The sheer number of the needy here is astonishing.

When distribution ends for the day, we join the other volunteers for lunch and are each given a large box of frozen pizza rolls before leaving for

Marietta. I feel guilty accepting mine, even though it comes from a partially distributed shipment that can't be put back into cold storage. My box eventually finds a home in my freezer, but, between its size and its source, I'm not sure I'll be able to bring myself to eat it.

I have no place to be on Tuesday until our clinical-medicine test at noon. It turns out to be difficult and covers some material we didn't think we were responsible for just yet. As with all our tests, it's gone in a flash, and now it's time to focus on the new material ahead.

We have a guest lecturer this afternoon, an allergist about my age, for whom I have considerable empathy. He has discarded what, for him, is our unfamiliar classroom technology. Instead he's going to use thirty-five-millimeter slides and speak from notes written on two legal pads. People presented like that when I was in my twenties, but to my classmates, this must be like watching black-and-white TV after a lifetime of high definition.

If only we could give him one of those classic, old, wooden pointers with a rubber tip at one end and an eyelet on the other for hanging it next to some dusty green chalkboard. Then, not only would his throwback ensemble be complete, but he might also feel at home. Unfortunately all we have is a laser pointer, and handing it to him turns out to be like giving a microwave oven to a pilgrim.

He has never used a pointer like this one, and it might just as well have fallen from the sky. Try as he might, he can't quite get the hang of it. He leaves it on as he walks around the podium, gesturing with his hands. All the while, the pointer's beam gyrates wildly around the darkened room, sometimes landing on a student, or causing bright flashes when it strikes reflectors in the darkened light fixtures overhead. What happens next is probably not one of our class's finest moments.

A strange game of laser tag breaks out, somehow without attracting the speaker's attention. When the light lands on a student as if it were a sniper's beam, he pretends to hurl himself to the floor to avoid an imaginary bullet. Other students take out their own pocket pointers and shine them back at the speaker's heart. Somehow through it all, I manage to learn something about allergies.

Wednesday is the first day of our Advanced Cardiac Life Support class at the hospital. Besides us, the ACLS class is made up of hospital staff and local paramedics. A mix of lectures and skill stations are designed to give us a chance to learn more about medications and EKG interpretation, as well as demonstrate our skills managing cardiac emergencies.

One of the skill stations demonstrates intubation, the placement of a breathing tube in a patient's trachea. To be fair, this class isn't designed to teach intubation, but many of the students are curious nonetheless. And, for some reason, the nurse at this station isn't being particularly helpful today.

During a break, a paramedic from a local ambulance service and I start taking small groups of our friends to the station, while the instructor watches passively from a few feet away. We guide the students through the intubation process, and then each tries their skill. Occasionally the mannequin's jaw clicks, indicating that too much pressure is being placed on the teeth.

"You're teaching them *wrong*," growls the preceptor.

Maybe, but at least we're trying, I think to myself. "Oh?" I ask innocently.

"They're putting *too* much *pressure* on the *teeth*," she retorts. "That's *wrong!*"

"Well, let's just let them get the tube in the right place once or twice. Then they can learn the niceties," I answer as politely as I can. She shakes her head in disgust and walks away. The impromptu training continues.

There is another rite of passage tonight; we've been invited to our first "drug dinner." From what I can gather, these dinners are fairly common. A pharmaceutical representative brings in a physician to speak about the benefits of a particular drug. Tonight it's a blood-pressure medication. The lecture is interesting, and I'm surprised that I can follow it. I'm not so sure I could have just a few months ago.

Thursday's only planned activity is a pharmacology lecture. When it ends, Tim calls a special meeting. This time it's for both genders, and no special clothing is required. We're puzzled until Tim starts talking about the clinical-medicine test we took two days ago. He's upset because the top grade was only a seventy-eight, and he wonders why we did so poorly. I decide to keep my mouth shut for a change, but others offer their own perspectives, including the fact that the test covered some material we didn't think we were responsible for at the time.

Tim doesn't buy the argument and starts to light into us just as Gloria enters the room. She calmly interjects, "It's not the class's problem, it's the faculty's problem." A new test will be developed, and we'll take it after spring break. I guess that some books will be coming home after all.

We're free to spend the rest of what feels like the first real spring afternoon preparing for tomorrow's ACLS exam. I take a short walk in the sunshine before Stan and Drew come over for a review. We give each other scenarios and come up with what interventions we would perform. Then, since it is St. Patrick's Day, we take on Harmar's huge, $6.95, corned-beef-and-cabbage special with Jan and her husband, Jonathan.

Friday's ACLS exam involves exercises at various skill stations. We're done by one o'clock in the afternoon and scatter for spring break. A newly tanned Drew is leaving for Florida with Jodi to relax and plan their spring wedding. Soon Stan, RaeAnn, Kathy, and I are on our way back to Columbus, where they'll stay at our house overnight before boarding flights for Colorado, North Dakota, and Chicago, respectively.

After dinner, Linda and I take our guests to the Marble Slab for the obligatory oversize ice-cream dessert. We've had more than enough milestones lately to justify celebrating with some ice cream. By mid-morning Saturday, my guests have scattered, and this old guy is ready for his own spring break.

CHAPTER 22

SPRING BREAK

It's probably no surprise that this particular spring break has not involved my going to the beach to meet girls. As I recall, that usually didn't work out all that well anyway. As my friend Bruce said at the time, "Why is it that, when we're in groups of two, they're in groups of three?" Awkward. Us, I mean.

I spend most of this break with family and friends. With only about two months left in my year away, I notify the generous souls who loaned me spare furniture that their chickens will soon be coming back home to roost:

I can either bring your stuff back to you, or dispose of it in Marietta, or some combination thereof.

Al: I'm not sure I'd want to be around Louise if you say you want your old leather chair back! On the other hand, visiting classmates rush to see who gets to sit in it first.

Homework continues over the break. Aside from studying for our clinical medicine do-over, there are short papers to be written about each of the few hundred diseases that will be covered on our board exam next year. That makes about two dozen for each of us to write by the end of the term. Stan e-mailed to say that he had just written one on the oral disease leukoplakia. I've already written that paper, too, so somehow we seem to be writing the same ones. Hopefully we can get that straightened out before there's much rework to be done.

Our family comes over for an early Easter dinner, and, by mid-afternoon, the break is over. I pick up RaeAnn and Kathy at the airport. RaeAnn's luggage has been lost and, unfortunately, so has Stan. Somehow he's being creatively rerouted from Colorado to Ohio via Boston and won't land here until eleven o'clock tonight. Kim, who always seems to be around to help with stragglers, will pick him up on her way through town.

CHAPTER 23

STUDENT ATHLETE

Marietta, Monday, March 28

I have a few minutes to talk with Stan after a rerun of our ill-fated clinical-medicine exam. He did start writing from my list of disease papers, but, fortunately, he's a great procrastinator and didn't get too far. We split up the remaining topics, and there are only a few extra ones for each of us to do.

I visit Bonnie for her mini-mental exam in the afternoon and learn that she didn't have a particularly good holiday. She just returned from a ten-day ICU stay for septic shock but is, nevertheless, in great spirits. She was able to go to church for Easter, and today is her younger brother's birthday.

We go into a quiet room for an exam that shows Bonnie to be a little disoriented with some memory loss, but in fairly good shape for all that she's been through. We say our good-byes, and I arrange to come back next month for depression screening.

After nearly ten months on campus, I usually feel at home, but there are times when I feel like I'm on another planet. Like tonight, when I read an all-campus e-mail about something called a "womyn's" program:

> Womyn With Wings, a choreopoem by J.H. Chapmyn will be presented. This choreopoem with music celebrates the strong, resilient, and powerful womyn who teach us how to fly. The performance is full of hope, humor, and stories that warm the inner heart.

Please come out, all are welcome.

The women's movement made huge strides during my young-adult years. Like many men of the time, I picked up a few scars along the way, but I think I'm better for it. I'm happy to be the husband of a strong, independent partner, as well as the proud father of a daughter who has taken advantage of opportunities that were denied her mother and grandmothers. And sure, there is more to be done, but I ask Linda by e-mail, "What the heck is a 'womyn?'"

Her response: "My unoppressed sisters are 'womyn.' The rest of us are still women. The womyn call you 'oppressyrs.'"

This morning, Dr. Kruger's overview of male urogenital diseases comes complete with the strikingly maimed pictures you would expect from a horror movie aficionado. "If you liked my pictures today," he concludes with a smile, "then you'll really enjoy my lecture on sexually transmitted diseases later this week."

One of today's guest lecturers gives us a glimpse of the future of surgery. Many vascular procedures, like repairing aneurysms and such, traditionally have been "open," involving opening the chest or abdomen. In many instances, surgeons are moving to "closed" procedures, using implants passed in through arteries and then assembled in place. This shortens recovery and cuts the risk for infection.

Seren announces that our volleyball team will have its first game tomorrow night. We're cleverly calling ourselves the "ACE Inhibitors," a takeoff on a class of blood-pressure medications. (Medical geekdom is alive and well.) I'll be playing this time, so the reawakening of my long dormant college intramural career is close at hand.

Passing the Quadranaou on my after-dinner walk this evening, I note that it now wears the trappings of my fourth and final season here. Children play baseball in the meadow below its ancient mound. I would like to stay and watch for a while, but there's another test in the morning.

Wednesday finds me up early and studying from behind a cup of coffee and an English muffin. Besides this being a test day, it's also the eighth anniversary of the passing of an old friend and kindred spirit. Pat Hughes and I used to encourage each other in our personal-development activities. We eventually both translated our dreams into self-employment, and our two businesses even got a chance to work together once.

Besides enthusiasm, Pat also had breast cancer. She seemed to beat it several times, going into periods of remission. As she often phrased it, she "had the breast cancer assignment" in life and used it to become one of our community's leading voices for cancer research.

The cancer eventually spread to her liver, but—outwardly at least—she maintained her sense of humor. The last time I saw her was at one of our periodic lunches just a few weeks before she died. A few months shy of her fiftieth birthday, she was still busy with her assignment. She had nearly completed a parody of a Paul Simon song, which she entitled "50 Ways to Leave Your Liver." Her goal was to use the song to raise money for cancer research. She already had a local singer lined up to record it.

Pat drew a cartoon for me that day, a picture of a smiling mouse, inscribed with the admonition to "be sillier." The drawing is still with me, here in my apartment, framed on a bookshelf alongside my desk.

I buy a pot of daffodils in Pat's memory about this time every year, and they eventually find their way to a growing garden at our house. This year's flowers are with me when I meet some classmates at a local tavern. We raise a toast to Pat, who would very much have approved of this adventure.

I later join Joe Kruger at the Marietta Brewery, where I have still more beer and snacks, along with some adult, male companionship. About the only thing that ever seems to get Joe down is college politics, from which we students are fairly well isolated. Joe is in a particularly good mood today, recounting how he helped test security as an air force physician at a Strategic Air Command base in northern Michigan. He was fortunate that it was only his ambulance that took a bullet from a flight-line guard.

Our volleyball match follows, and it isn't long before I start to doubt that beer and heavy hors d'oeuvres at two different restaurants were my wisest pregame choices. We end up losing two games to one. It's fun to be playing again, but I'm definitely slower than I remember. No one seems to mind my style of play, if you can call repeatedly knocking the ball into the next court a "style."

Our team stops at Seren's after the match for even more beer and food. I end up turning in after midnight, not at all sure how my classmates live like this on a regular basis. On the other hand, I've been true to Pat's advice to be sillier.

The next morning is Dr. Kruger's much-anticipated lecture on sexually transmitted diseases. As one might have expected, it's factual and organized, describing the various diseases, symptoms, and treatments. But, of course, what we have really been waiting for are the pictures Joe promised, and he doesn't let us down. Some are of patients with such horrible cases that it's difficult even to identify gender.

Speaking of pictures, we get our own taken on Friday, this time wearing our white coats. These will be sent to our future clinical preceptors, presumably so they can recognize us when we show up on their doorsteps in a few months. The pictures also will be posted on a bulletin board here at school. Even now, the class ahead of us has such a board, complete with pictures of bright, smiling faces and captions indicating which clinical rotation each student is currently on.

Linda is visiting family in Maryland this weekend, and I drive through to London for a night with the 2 Unit crew. After dinner, we're called to a nearby state prison for an injured inmate.

As with most of our prisoner patients, he's well behaved and forthcoming with answers to our questions. To put his behavior in perspective, it should be noted that he's wearing a bright-orange jumpsuit, his hands and feet are shackled, we have an armed guard on board with us, and another follows closely behind in a white pickup. The guards even carry a preprinted escape poster, complete with the inmate's picture and description, so that they can quickly alert local police in case he somehow manages to give us the slip.

Tonight's prisoner, an unfortunate young man in his early twenties, was supposed to be released from prison tomorrow. Instead, for some reason unknown to us, the other inmates in his cellblock beat him in his sleep and fractured his jaw. He's just a week younger than my son Daniel, my personal yardstick for deciding who in this world is still young. Apparently that was old enough for him to have gotten into trouble and serve out his sentence.

We're also called out for a run to a home far out in the country, where we find a thirty-six-year-old woman lying bent at the waist on the sofa. Her husband and son are sitting nearby. She tells us that she ate about six hours ago and soon after started having severe pain in the right upper quadrant of her abdomen, along with nausea. Other than her obvious discomfort, we don't find much unusual about her appearance or vital signs. She is a diabetic, but her blood-sugar level is normal. She needs to go to the hospital, so we start an IV on the way and give her some medication to calm the nausea.

I'm back in Marietta on Sunday morning for my second ER shift. I feel less like a stranger this time, and there is considerable variety among our patients today. A couple brings in three children covered with poison ivy. A man has severe abdominal pain from Crohn's disease. A woman learns she has a tumor behind her bladder. This new career seems a good mix of science, intuition, and the chance to help people.

Linda stops by for an overnight stay on her way back from Maryland. We have dinner together and then watch a video she shot at her mother's farm over the weekend. My brother-in-law Ted, who loves being the family foil, is comically bemoaning his small chin in one scene. "It's the only thing that keeps me from being totally perfect," he whimpers to the camera. Then he holds up a small statuette of a weasel and asks, "OK, which one of us has the smaller chin?"

From off camera, his younger brother Kerry pipes up, "The real question is, which one of you is the real weasel?"

Marietta, Monday, April 4

Linda is still asleep this morning, and Skyler literally dogs my footsteps as I get ready for school. I rejoin them after morning classes, and, before they leave for home, they walk me back to campus, past trees now flowering in the sun.

I'm up early Tuesday to review for a test that is followed by a guest speaker on orthopedic emergencies. Dr. Kruger would likely approve of the many pictures of mangled limbs. Miranda follows him with a lecture on birth control. Once again, I feel ancient. I used to know all about birth control options, but no longer. The rest of the class looks bored; they know most of this stuff already.

We have a urine-analysis lab Wednesday. We're using our own pee, and I'm happy to report that mine is doing just fine. We run various dip tests and then spin it down to isolate any floating debris. A classmate announces— without the slightest trace of self-consciousness—that she has a urinary tract infection, and we take turns looking at abnormalities in her urine.

My nightly e-mail includes a family-wide broadcast from Linda:

Hi all,

I came across this quote today. I like it and thought that you might too.

"Real joy comes not from ease or riches or from the praise of men, but from doing something worthwhile."

—Sir Wilfred Grenfell
English missionary & physician (1865–1940)

Stan drops by after school Thursday to watch a hockey game. Colorado College, in his hometown of Colorado Springs, is playing in the NCAA Frozen Four in Columbus. Unfortunately for Stan, Colorado College loses, but overnight he and RaeAnn somehow get tickets to Friday's finals. Each has a dog in the fight: RaeAnn went to the University of North Dakota, and the University of Denver is at least in Stan's home state. I wish the hockey fans safe travels and head home for the weekend.

There's a guest waiting for me: young Mr. Patrick. We're babysitting while his parents have a rare dinner alone. It's also the start of another month, and so it's time to check on our financial plan. Daniel and Gary aren't quite ready to move out of the condo that they rent from us. We had been planning on selling it this year, so it's time for another midcourse correction.

Rich, our next-door neighbor, stops by on Saturday morning for some help with his mother's computer, and, after a few hours, it's computing again. It's nice to do something for him for a change, as he and his garage full of tools have bailed us out many a time over the last twenty-odd years. He even once helped me replace a water heater on Thanksgiving, finishing just before our guests arrived.

I have to leave early Sunday to get back to school. One of our guest speakers, a radiologist, offered to let us watch him read X-rays, and today is my day. I'm at the hospital by nine that morning and find him very open to questions, telling me what he sees and, sometimes, even how he sees it. It's amazing what he can pick up in just a few seconds.

Linda calls mid-morning to break some bad news: yet another family water heater has bit the dust. This time it's the one in Daniel's condo; I knew it was time to sell that place. Once again, Rich rushes to the rescue, spending his day off helping Linda pick out a replacement and then installing it himself. So I stayed square in my debt to him for a whole twenty-four hours. It's a blessing having a saint with tools living next door.

Marietta, Monday, April 11

I'm up early this morning for a test, and then our case team meets to review an imaginary retired accountant suffering from gradual weight loss. Test grades have been posted by the time our meeting is over, but I forgo learning mine until tomorrow. Instead, I take a peaceful walk home past the old mansions, their lawns now dotted with new purple blooms.

I have another shift in the ER this afternoon, this time working with Dr. Butler, a young resident. We have several patients during the afternoon and early evening. A boy has dislocated his finger playing basketball. The pleasant demeanor of a sixty-five-year-old man masks the seriousness of his kidney failure. And, in something of overkill, a rescue squad brings in a young girl with a sore throat.

It's unseasonably cool Wednesday when our case teams meet to present our mock patients. Our team's retired accountant has now had the colonoscopy we ordered, and, unfortunately, it was positive for cancer. Our proposed treatment involves removal of at least a portion of his colon.

Spring returns on Thursday, and Miranda presents some of the procedures we may be called on to perform during our emergency-medicine clinical rotations. Our current ER shifts are designed primarily to develop our diagnostic and patient interaction skills; the clinical rotations that start this summer will be far more hands-on. Miranda covers lumbar punctures, placing arterial lines, and inserting nasogastric tubes. I pay close attention, partly because it's a career area I've been interested in, and partly because procedures have been always a challenge for me.

Everybody has his or her own self-image. A part of mine—liberally substantiated by history, I might add—is the belief that I'm something of a klutz. I wasn't the most agile of athletes; I did, after all, step on my own track shoes. I have never had the neatest penmanship, and I'm not the smoothest of dancers. Instead I'm someone who finds new bruises in the shower and wonders what I bumped into this time. With that kind of history, it's no wonder medical procedures have sometimes been a challenge. I eventually become proficient, but I'm hardly a natural.

Some of my classmates in EMT school could start intravenous lines successfully nearly every time. I had to practice for days, repeatedly using one hand to stick a needle into pieces of paper at just the right angle. Some paramedic students were naturals who could accurately place breathing tubes in their sleep. (A handy skill for those pesky cardiac arrests at two in the morning.) Before I was ready to intubate a live patient—under the watchful eyes of an anesthesiologist in an operating room—I practiced for hours with a plastic dummy at the squad bay. My goal was to successfully intubate the mannequin fifty times in a row. If I missed an attempt, I started all over again.

Speaking of finding bruises in the shower, somehow I have managed to scrape my elbow, and now it's infected. I take advantage of the college's infirmary, where a fellow mid-level health-care provider—a nurse practitioner—treats me. It's the first time I've been treated like a health-care professional, and it's an interesting experience. I have the wound drained and cultured and also get some antibiotics.

Stan was motivated by Miranda's talk today, and he's decided to read up on some of the procedures. Later, he sends me an e-mail about it:

I was reading the procedures from the primary care book. That book really made things kind of clear. I wish I had time to really read it, but that's not gonna happen...

Hope your cellulitis check-up went well. We should drain it in class.

Cellulitis is no surprise, Keflex [the prescribed drug], also not a surprise... Remember: it is renally eliminated, and cephalosporins are pregnancy category B. It also passes through breast milk, so you might want to hold off for a bit...

Friday is a perfect seventy-degree spring day that starts with two endocrine lectures and then one on legal issues surrounding the PA profession. When classes end, our case team meets to discuss our next simulated patient, a thirty-five-year-old country-club manager suffering from panic attacks.

I'm back in Westerville on Saturday morning, where Linda and I are working on her park project at Otterbein Lake. This morning, volunteers are making depth measurements to help engineers design some of the park's features. It's a pleasant spring day, and the crew is having a good time. Some are in boats equipped with sonar devices, while others wade with measuring poles nearer to shore. I record readings radioed—or sometimes just shouted—from across the water. The deepest spot in the lake turns out to be about fifteen feet.

I'm back in Marietta Sunday for an all-day ER shift. Today's crew consists of Dr. Butler, three nurses, and me. Among our patients are quite a few sick kids, but we also have our share of accident victims. One child was in a bike accident. A woman brings in her dehydrated daughter, who added to her troubles by falling on the way here. Most of our patients are pleasant, easy-to-talk-to, salt-of-the-earth types. I discover telling little children that I'm a grandpa sometimes helps.

A mother brings in two hyperactive children with chicken pox. The kids are in perpetual motion, finding lots to play with in the exam room. At one point, they even try to hang from ceiling-mounted IV hooks. They remind me of the twins Daniel used to play with as a child. They could be so frenetic that I called them Thing One and Thing Two, after characters in a Dr. Seuss story. Now they're both grown and in medical school.

One of our patients today turns out to be a drug seeker. I knew these guys existed, but I'd never met one in the ER before. He's an odd young man who complains of a mysterious cough, yet, during the thirty-odd minutes I spend with him, I never actually see him coughing. Hmm. We prescribe the industrial-strength version of an over-the-counter cough suppressant. He calls later, upset that there aren't any narcotics in the medication.

The procession of the sick and injured continues: a man in congestive heart failure; another with a sore back; an ill baby; a girl with a stiff neck and fever, who, fortunately, doesn't have meningitis; and a little boy with a barking cough, who, fortunately, doesn't have pertussis. Dr. Butler tells me that, in this county alone, five children have been diagnosed with pertussis in just the past month.

By the end of the shift, my feet are tired, and I'm ready to relax. Our volleyball team is in the play-offs tonight, but I don't really have the energy to play. I doubt that they'll miss my athletic prowess anyway. Instead, I relax on my front steps with a cup of coffee, enjoying the late afternoon sunshine. I think about having been nineteen and playing defensive end on my dorm's team, with friends whose names I have mostly forgotten. This final chapter of my intramural athletic career may not have been stellar, but I enjoyed it anyway. I've enjoyed them all.

CHAPTER 24

SPRINGTIME ON CAMPUS

Marietta, Monday, April 18

The weather is becoming more spring-like as the weeks roll by. After an early-morning test and lectures on endocrine diseases, I'm off to Izzy's for a sandwich at one of their outside tables.

Speaking of sandwiches, today I'm sandwiched in the lunch line between the college's president and its provost. Both take the time to say hello. Even a minimal greeting probably wouldn't have taken place at the much-larger universities I attended in my youth. For the record, the president is also having the chicken sandwich, but she skips the lettuce and instead orders fries.

We spend several hours discussing skin diseases on a warm Tuesday. I find dermatology especially difficult because two patients with different-looking skin lesions still can end up having the same disease. When classes let out for the day, it's a classic eighty-degree afternoon that reminds any former student of what springtime has always meant on a college campus.

Back in our dorm complex at the University of Maryland, spring was a special time. Students came alive after being cooped up all winter. On a day like this one, music would blare from stereo speakers propped in open windows. Guys would catch Frisbees, toss baseballs, and try to strike up conversations with passing girls. I'm not doing any of those things today, but, still, it feels good to be on a campus when the warm, lengthening days seem especially full of promise.

We have lectures on emergency medicine and orthopedics for the rest of the week. By Friday night, I'm back in London and sharing dinner with the rest of the crew. Just as we finish eating, we're dispatched on an unknown emergency. Unlike a typical run, we don't know the chief complaint, sex, or age of our patient, so we can't prepare mentally on the way. These calls are often just accidental 9-1-1 hang-ups, but not this time.

We arrive at a garden-style apartment. The door is locked, and we can't get anyone's attention inside, so we have the police force it open. A few steps into the apartment, we hear a man's voice calling out. We find him lying on the floor of a small bathroom, trapped under the body of a lifeless woman. She is cyanotic, cool to the touch, and not breathing. The man is profoundly distraught and repeatedly wailing, "My baby is gone!"

We quickly move our patient into the hallway so that we have more room to work. She doesn't have a pulse, so we start CPR, but her chances don't look good. The man calms down enough to tell his story. His wife is in her early forties and has no obvious injuries, but she does have a weak heart and a history of cancer. He last spoke with her this morning before leaving for work. She was in the bathroom when he came home tonight, and he took a nap. She hadn't come out an hour later, so he investigated and found her unresponsive. He tried to move the large woman by himself after calling 9-1-1, and apparently she fell on him.

While CPR continues, we connect the heart monitor and find the extremely slow rhythm referred to as agonal because it is too slow to support life. Unfortunately it isn't anything that can be fixed with our defibrillator. We continue CPR, start an IV, begin cardiac medications, and place a breathing tube. We've gone through the prescribed rounds of medications by the time we get to the hospital, and, shortly after our arrival, the attending physician pronounces our patient dead.

Runs like this aren't satisfying, but it's a common outcome. At least the family can have some peace of mind in knowing that everything that could have been done was done. And, after our own disappointment passes, we will feel the same way.

It takes a while to clean and restock our truck back at the station. I eventually crawl back into bed with earplugs to block out Steve's snoring and the roar of large fans that this crew likes in its bunk room. The background noise eventually inspires a dream about flying in a World War II bomber.

My bomber lands at six in the morning after an uneventful segment of sleep, and I'm out the door and on my way home as soon as my day-shift replacement arrives. Linda and I meet for breakfast and then spend a quiet

Saturday at home while large, wet snowflakes fall. It may be mid-April, but the Ohio winter is still not quite through with us.

Tonight, along with most of our family, we're at Al and Louise's for a traditional Passover dinner. We've been coming here for this meal for at least twenty years, and the familiarity is comforting. Louise again has made enough of several different entrees so that if twice as many guests were to show up and all decide to eat the same thing, there would still be more than enough food to go around. As usual, no one leaves hungry.

After catching up on some household chores, Linda and I are off to Starbucks on Sunday morning. There, I come face to face with a childhood memory: a half-moon cookie. When my brother and I were young, our parents would take us to a local bakery where we would each get one of these half-white, half-brown, frosted treats. Today's cookies inspire us to share other memories from our childhoods.

Marietta, Monday, April 25

I hope it wasn't the half-moon cookie, but I start the school week under the weather. I go in anyway, and I'm a bit better by mid-afternoon. Stan exchanges an e-mail with his "little brother," a student in the new class that will be sitting in our seats starting in June:

> We just heard today that you folks were officially fired into the mix. Well enough of the formal stuff. Basically, I want to say nice job getting in, the hard part is over, now you just gotta be yourself...

I sleep like the dead, and, even after nine hours of sleep, it's still only five in the morning. I feel much better and take advantage of the extra time to study. An overnight drizzle is ending as I make my way to school. During a break later on, I hand over my last rent check and make arrangements to move out next month. All that is left to do now is rent a truck and see which of our sons can help me on moving day.

Lunch is two burgers at McDonald's, which is all that really sounds good right now. That is followed by a lecture on orthopedics and reading X-rays. We learn the stylized mantra of the radiologist, who may pick up an X-ray and dictate something like, "I see the pelvic view of a skeletally mature female with symmetric hip joints, normal bowel gases, and..."

My family is coming to town for Mother's Day, so my mission after school on Wednesday is to find a restaurant for the occasion. I finally decide on the *Becky Thatcher*, the stern-wheeler/restaurant permanently docked in Marietta. Linda and I ate there with Joe Kruger and his wife, and the small bar in its bow has become one of our class's after-hours haunts.

I use a break Thursday to visit Bonnie at the nursing home and screen her for depression. She's in a great mood and just had her hair done. Her mind is working well, and she's able to answer questions easily. A salt-of-the-earth lady, she tells me more about her life, covering her late boyfriend and her family.

This is my last scheduled visit with Bonnie, and I've enjoyed our time together. I hope that I'll get back to see her before I leave town. In spite of my good intentions, though, I know that life will stay busy, and it's unlikely I'll make it back. Like so many experiences I've had this year, this one is fleeting, and I'm grateful for all it has taught me.

Friday I'm up at three in the morning, again for absolutely no good reason, and I can't get back to sleep. I finally bite the bullet and get up, start the coffee, warm up a bagel, peer out into the rainy night, and settle in for some early studying. One advantage to living alone is that I'm not disturbing anyone, even at this hour. If I were at home, Skyler would be on me in an instant, excited about the prospect of an early breakfast.

We have a ninety-minute break after a test, which is more than enough time for Stan and me to devour a huge breakfast of eggs, bacon, and pancakes at the Harmar. I guess my appetite is back. We have a lecture on abnormal pregnancies after breakfast. We've had many opportunities to marvel at the human body this year, but, to me, fetal development is especially mysterious.

If you wanted to build a house, you would hire trained crews and give them detailed plans. The construction tasks would be completed in an order that optimizes efficiency. Utilities—like electricity, gas, and water—would get turned on fairly late in the game, because the house itself doesn't need them; the people who move in will.

Building a baby is different in so many ways, starting with the plan being coded in DNA and executed by molecules. Utilities—like oxygen, nutrition, and waste removal—have to be provided, in one form or another, from the outset because the cells are alive. Each day, the developing fetus is slightly different than it was the day before. Besides getting some services from its mother, it gradually begins to depend on its own systems.

I believe in God—and evolution, too, by the way. This year, I've had a chance to learn more about the body and its mechanisms, and, the more I learn, the more magical and harmonious it all seems. The engineer in me is amazed, and I find it hard to dismiss the hand of a really good systems architect in all of this.

We're up early Saturday for the long-awaited golf scramble. A light rain is falling as we set up. My main job today will be cooking lunch for our guests on large charcoal grills with Julia. She used to work in a restaurant and quickly takes charge. While she starts the grills, I'm pressed into service as the beer-cart driver, going from hole to hole in what has turned into a healthy downpour. As a nongolfer, I didn't realize golfers would drink beer at nine in the morning while playing in a cold rain. They will.

The rain finally stops, I rejoin what Julia refers to as the "grill dogs," and we start cooking chicken and hot dogs. It's fun working with her because she seems to be enjoying herself so much. Other classmates work indoors, baking side dishes and waiting tables in the clubhouse. We have about sixty mouths to feed, and the golfers have a good time. By the time we're done, we've raised about $2,500 for our class and local flood relief.

I'm cold and wet, and the first order of business back at the apartment is to take a long, hot shower and put on some dry clothes. Linda and Skyler show up later in the afternoon. We leave Skyler in charge and walk downtown for dinner at a small restaurant on the banks of the Ohio. The Levee House is in a 180-year-old structure with a good view of the riverbank, not far from where passenger-laden stern-wheelers used to dock. It feels like we're on vacation.

After Linda leaves on Sunday, I settle in to study in front of an open window that lets in the spring air. Eventually the weather wins out over the books, and I take a walk, starting out down Fourth Street, past the mansions. It's the same route I took in June, when I was exploring Marietta for the first time. I've taken this route many times since, as Marietta gradually became my second home.

Making a right turn toward downtown, I pass the army-recruiting station and several storefronts, before turning right again on Third Street, back toward home. I pass the fire station, where the crew cleaning their engine pauses and waves.

From Stan:

This week is crying for Empire Buffet.

Holla, su bocca es muy grande con queso!!!!!!!!!!!!!!!! (I have no idea what that has to do with.)

Hey! Does anyone have the finally tally as to what is on this upcoming exam...don't tell me "all the female stuff"—that answer sucked.

CHAPTER 25
THE TOWN I ALREADY MISS

Marietta, Monday, May 2

The campus is noticeably quieter because, aside from graduating seniors, we're the only ones who haven't already left for the summer. The stage is nearly set for the next class to take our places for their own year of adventure.

More of our training these days is in preparation for clinical rotations that start next month, and today I'm off to Selby General for a surgical orientation. With three surgical rotations coming up, I had better learn my way around an operating room. We're taught the various roles of the OR staff, and our trainers show us the right way to wash our hands and step into sterile gowns.

Most members of the operating-room team are gloved by others. Someone already in sterile garb holds the gloves open, and the person to be gloved just shoves his or her freshly scrubbed hands in. Our nurse instructors tell us that it would be best if we could glove ourselves without help, and then they try to show us how.

I ask for my usual extra-large gloves for this exercise, but all they have are mediums. First, I grip the left glove in my right hand, using the cuff of my gown's right sleeve to protect the glove from my bare right hand. Next, I try to worm my left hand down the left sleeve and into the waiting glove. Try as I might, I can't get the too-small glove to stretch enough to let my hand in. My first surgical rotation is months away, but, at this rate, I might still be standing here. I'll have to practice later on my own, with larger gloves.

Later in the day, our case team meets with a faculty member who is playing all the roles associated with our final case. It's that of an elderly woman who fell in her bathtub and was brought to the emergency room complaining of hip pain. While the complaint suggests X-rays to look for fractures, we also need to look at the rest of the picture to figure out why she might have fallen in the first place.

A squad brought our patient in, so I decide to show some respect for my EMS brothers and sisters by asking to speak with the paramedic in charge. We learn what the medic saw in the patient's home. Our problem list grows as we investigate further. We now suspect that she has a chronic lung condition, anemia, arthritis, depression, and alcoholism.

It may be the first Tuesday in May, but there is a thin coat of frost on my car this morning. Most of our day is spent on dermatology, and, when we've finished, I walk part of the way home with Stan. He plans to go for a run and then find an empty room on campus to study. Back at my apartment, I change into some comfortable jeans and get back to my books. Eventually my stomach starts to growl, so I make some spaghetti and picnic in front of the TV.

After classes on Wednesday, Joe Kruger and I take one of our periodic trips to the Marietta Brewery. He regales me with problems he's having trying to plan his daughter's wedding. I tell him the nice thing about wedding plans is that the guests will never know what was *supposed* to happen. Our daughter's wedding cake was destroyed in transit, and the restaurant scrambled to find enough replacement cake for three hundred people at a nearby grocery. Some guests still assume they had a piece of what was actually a small Styrofoam prop cake used in the wedding photos.

While we've been talking, some graduating seniors have entered wearing T-shirts emblazoned with the words "Bar Crawl." Joe tells me this is a senior tradition. Seniors go from bar to bar during their last week on campus, spending their last few minutes in each before graduation.

A warm, sunny Thursday starts with a lecture on vitamins and herbs. Stan, Drew, and I meet later at the Empire Buffet for lunch and then settle in for an afternoon of lectures on endocrine diseases. I study after school, but eventually the seventy-degree weather lures me out for a walk.

On a whim I go to our classroom area. Several classmates in the computer room start to hide beer bottles until they realize the middle-aged guy with salt-and-pepper hair is just me. An impromptu Cinco de Mayo celebration has broken out in the midst of working on their theses. They're young, it's spring, the term is ending soon, and there is a holiday somewhere to celebrate. I don't blame them a bit.

Many of us meet later in the small bar in the bow of the *Becky Thatcher*. It's noisy tonight, with music, a large crowd, and waitresses carrying pails of bottled Corona. Tim's e-mail tonight pretty well sums up our mood:

Keep up the good work; the light is getting brighter by the day.

After a day filled with lectures on eye diseases, leukemia, and lymphoma, I spend a rare Friday night in town at a cookout at Jeff's apartment. I bring along the requisite six-pack to share. It's a familiar college experience; the weekend stretches out in front of us, and the end of the term is approaching.

Linda shows up Saturday, and we walk around town, enjoying the warm, spring afternoon and dinner outside under an umbrella-shaded table at an Italian restaurant. The next morning, we start Mother's Day with coffee on the front steps while we watch the town come to life. From houses behind blooming gardens, people in their Sunday best are on their way to take mothers and grandmothers out for lunch.

The rest of our family arrives just before lunch. Katie, Tom, and Patrick are here, along with Gary. Daniel has to work at the radio station, so he can't be with us today. It's their first glimpse of my apartment in a while, and they find their pictures on my mantle. Gary and I case out the place, deciding which items we'll take out through which doors when he comes back to help me move in a few weeks. Later we have lunch on the *Becky Thatcher* while coal barges motor by, heading downriver in the afternoon sun.

Marietta, Monday, May 9

The week begins with lectures on brain injuries and other neurological problems. It's followed by a two-day Pediatric Advanced Life Support course at the hospital. We also have our final pharmacology lecture and thank Dr. Waller's two-dimensional image on our screen. He has been helpful all term, including timely e-mail answers to our questions at all hours of the day. For those of us who expect to end up in a medical practice, he has given us many of the tools of our new trade.

One of my dinners this week is hot dogs and popcorn at the college's baseball stadium, Pioneer Park. Marietta squares off against Otterbein College in the first game of the league championship series. It's the only intercollegiate sporting event I've managed to see all year. I have mixed allegiances since Otterbein is in our hometown and it's Daniel's alma mater. I feel more like a dad again tonight when I go back to the car for a quilt to keep the women in our group warm.

Our nuclear family today. From left: Daniel, Linda, Katie, me, Gary.

Friday's weekend trip home will be my last. Besides the usual cargo, I take along some of the things I won't need here anymore, including a suit, my squad uniform, and some remaining winter clothing. I return Sunday with tools to disassemble furniture, along with empty packing boxes and a camera.

With finals coming up, I spend most of the day studying. Late in the sunny afternoon, I take a break and drive to the Harmar side of the Muskingum River. There, from an overlook not far from Bonnie's nursing home, I can see all of Marietta spread out between the two rivers. There is the college over there, downtown, and the old port. Trees screen any view of my apartment.

Watching the city life below, I realize just how much I've enjoyed being part of it this year. Being here has also helped me remember long-forgotten details of earlier adventures. Like other places I've lived, there will always be memories for me here. But my life centers more on people than it does places, and most of those people won't be here. Like college towns everywhere, Marietta is really more like a theater stage, and a fresh crop of actors is on its way to take our places. Soon this will be their town.

I stand on the overlook for a few more minutes, taking pictures of the town I already miss.

CHAPTER 26

END GAME

Marietta, Monday, May 16

I've been trying to finish off my food supply before it's time to leave. That has already made for some strange meals, but none yet have included the box of shelf-stable pasta I bought on my first day in town. It will probably meet the same fate as my anatomy lab outfit: the dumpster behind my apartment.

And then, of course, there is the box of food-bank pizza rolls still kicking around unopened in my freezer. With time running out for the little fellows, I decide to bring them to school today. We have a test, and some of my classmates like to stay overnight and study in the classroom. That sounds like a terrible way to spend the night, but maybe they'll be hungry this morning.

Imagine my surprise when my pizza roll regifting scheme is not met with the gratitude I might have expected. Apparently everyone else has been eating these things for weeks. "Giving us pizza rolls is like giving fruitcakes at Christmas," Seren quips, playing into the legend that no new fruitcakes have been made in years. People just keep regifting the ones they get.

Joe Kruger's last lecture is on Tuesday. He has decided to go back to being a full-time hospital pathologist, so this will also be his last year in Marietta. Today he covers several nerve disorders that, hopefully, we'll never see, including mad cow, and gets a round of applause when he finishes. He has done a good job for us all year, including making presentations on topics he probably hadn't thought about in a long time.

I cross paths with Joe, his wife, and their daughter Kristen later, during my after-dinner walk. They invite me to Kristen's graduation party, and I happily accept. I also let Joe in on a decision I've made about the final in his class. The test is optional because he'll drop our lowest score. Given the math, no matter how well I might do on the test, I can't change my overall grade. There is only so much time left to study, and my grades are still up for grabs in other courses. I've decided to take his final, without studying, just to see what I still need to learn before our boards next year.

Joe is shocked. "I can't *believe* it!" he exclaims. He proceeds to tell me how he behaved after he took his medical boards. He just assumed that he had failed, went home, and immediately started studying all over again. He kept that up for several weeks, until he received word that he had passed after all. After listening to his story, I'm not surprised that he doesn't approve of my slightly less rabid approach to life. Oh well.

We have our last clinical diagnostics lecture Wednesday morning, after which I assemble yet another eclectic lunch from my rapidly diminishing stores. I meet Joe later for beer and dinner and tell him how much I've appreciated his lectures. And I'll miss our periodic trips to the Marietta Brewery for India pale ale and middle-aged adult camaraderie. Joe responds by critiquing me as a student. Apparently if I had asked one more question in class, he would have had to strangle me. Sorry, Joe, that's just who I am.

I resume preparations for finals after dinner. I'm on kind of a high and try to sum up my feelings in my nightly e-mail to family and friends:

> This year has been an incredible experience, and so too will be the 15 month clinical phase. I feel like I have won some kind of lottery, but as I think about it, that's been the case with most of my life. I am blessed to have been raised by loving parents who enabled me, to have married the perfect mate, and then to have had the greatest kids (and grandson). After that, everything else has been gravy.

There's a knock at the door, and I find Drew and Stan. Apparently they're on their own emotional highs and have brought along a six-pack. We end up drinking, snacking, talking, and laughing until well after midnight.

We have our last lectures Thursday and Friday, finishing up with pain management in the terminally ill and our case team's last presentation. I brought my camera and start snapping pictures. It's been a family tradition of ours to take pictures on the first day of school. Now I have one of me leaving school on what may be my last day of classes forever. It will serve as the other bookend to the one my mother took in 1951 on my first day of kindergarten.

Last day of classes, 2005.

Tonight's e-mail includes notes from old friends. One is from Bob, my old college roommate. I'll be seeing him soon, when he brings his racecar to a track near our home. Long before my life included Marietta, Stan and Drew, the Harmar Tavern, Killian's beer, and fried-bologna sandwiches, Bob and I would stop at The Other Room in College Park:

> Hope to see you in a couple of weeks. Congratulations. You should celebrate with a meatball sub and a Schlitz dark!

My last Saturday in Marietta is warm and sunny. I spend most of it studying but take a break for Joe's daughter's graduation party. Linda and I meet later at Adornetto's in Zanesville to celebrate the upcoming end of our separation. It's a treat to see her, watch her smile, and hear the laughter in her voice. This year has been exciting for me but lonely for her. We'll be home together again next week, and there will be no more exams for a while.

Linda brought me the weekly bills, and so my day ends at the computer, checkbook in hand. It's also my last monthly look at our financial plan before moving back home. There don't appear to be any major changes on the horizon. It will be nice to have money coming in again, but that won't be for another year and a half. Steady as she goes, oh financial ship of state.

I'm up on a soggy Sunday before sunrise, even without an alarm. Other than final trips to the Laundromat and grocery, I spend the day studying for finals. By nightfall, all I want to do is watch a show and go to bed. E-mails come flying in from similarly frazzled classmates scattered all over town. Stan sums up our mood:

> Just was thinking about you. You are the man...I hate studying.
> Shoot me now.

CHAPTER 27

MEMENTOS

Marietta, Monday, May 23

We have our first two finals today, and I get back to the apartment by mid-afternoon. I'm not sure how I did, but there is no time to agonize about it; this is my last chance to study for tomorrow's pharmacology final. The process of reviewing drug family trees is a grindingly familiar one by now.

Fortunately the phone rings and the grind can stop for a while. It's my "little sister" Adriana, whose family is in town helping her move into an apartment. Soon she will be starting her own summer anatomy boot camp. I can almost smell the preservative. I arrange to meet them for dinner and am no longer surprised to find that I'm older than her parents. They offer to take me to dinner, and I accept, conducting a brief tour of the city on the way.

"Is there an Applebee's around here?" her father asks.

"Yes, near the freeway," I answer. "Unless you'd like to try one of our local places."

"Hmm? A real college place?" he asks. Maybe he is recalling one of his own old haunts.

"It surely is," I reply. "And it will take you back." I know it has for me.

And so Adriana's dad has his first fried-bologna sandwich at the Harmar, and I have passed my home away from home on to the next wave of Marietta PA students. I'll miss the place, but I'm content that another class is about to have a similar experience.

Adriana is concerned she won't know anyone in her class. I remind her that everyone else is in the same boat, and her loneliness will end on the first day of anatomy. Someone will stand up to make the first cut, a team will be born, and her year will blossom from there. The work here has been painful at times, and I'm anxious for my clinical rotations to start. Still, answering Adriana's questions makes me think about everything she'll be experiencing in the coming year. And how I would do it all over again in a heartbeat.

From Stan:

It's 3 am, I finally woke up from the first real sleep in the past few days...missed my last appointment to the ER...guess I gotta go tomorrow instead. Dang, that was a good sleep...2 days till the end of the year BBQ...S— gotta play Command and Conquer...see ya.

I'm up Tuesday, convinced that our final starts at nine. Fortunately I look at the schedule in time to see it actually starts at eight, thus, narrowly avoiding a repeat of a mistake our daughter made in college. Katie slept though the start of her organic-chemistry final, sprinting to class in time to join it in progress. She passed.

Our grades for the first three exams are up later, and I did fine. I didn't retire to compete for grades, but, yes, my mind still works. We spend the afternoon filling out program evaluations. Afterward, I wander around downtown, looking for the perfect memento of my time here in the River City. Nothing seems appropriate.

We have a comprehensive final on Wednesday, but, after only a few minutes, the computers give us their final salute and crash. We're excused while the techies try to fix things. Jan and I use the time to walk to the Harmar for breakfast, where she tells me about her family over a giant meal of coffee, eggs, and pancakes. She grew up on a farm not far from Marietta, and her father was a coal miner. Her mother has gone back to school and is studying nursing at the same local community college where we had our blood and urine labs.

Our exam resumes, and, later, we're called in two at a time for our physical-exam final. Mine goes fine, and, just like that, the year is over. I'm now officially a new, second-year PA student. That title differentiates us from the old second years who will finish their rotations this summer and then graduate in August. I clean out my study carrel and turn in my still-mysterious ophthalmoscope.

Drew and I stop by the Alumni Office and get large posters of the college as mementos. I spend the rest of the day packing and disassembling furniture, while, all over town, my classmates are probably doing the same. Meanwhile Adriana and her soon-to-be friends are individually exploring the town, wondering what the coming year will hold for them.

What I remember most about my original college days were its intense, personal relationships. Like many men, most of my energy in the years since has gone into building a family and a career. I do have some close friends, but many of my adult relationships have been more superficial than those of my youth. Maybe that is why the reappearance of college friendships this year has been such a surprise for me.

I haven't dated or kept the hours of a twenty-something, but my life here has had much the same feel as college always had for me. Maybe it's because we've been preparing together for a future that is new, important, and unpredictable. Whatever the reason, I'm grateful for the privilege to have gone back in time.

We're still in the celebrating mood later at Applebee's, where the half-priced happy-hour drinks are flowing, and everyone is incredibly happy. We're all carded, including me. My classmates tease the waitress to check my ID very carefully because it's obviously a fake.

I settle in later for what will be my last night alone in the apartment. Even with the bare walls and growing pile of boxes, it's hard to believe that this part of the adventure is really over. Before turning in, I send a final note to my classmates:

> I'd like to thank you all for making me feel so much at home and—even though I'm so ancient—part of the group. Coming back to school has been one of the top few experiences of my life and, in no small measure, that's because of you. I only hope that you keep living your dreams, no matter how old you get along the way.

Our final task of the year is to perform physicals the next morning for four- and five-year-olds who will be entering school this fall. We work to establish rapport with the kids, and some of their parents ask if we're going to stay in the area so they could bring their children to us in the future. It's an enjoyable and humbling experience.

Linda arrives in time for Aaron's end-of-school party. The event is a sweet one, with lots of laughter and a fair amount of drinking. RaeAnn asks to have her picture taken with me because I've been her Dad away from home.

My Internet connection will be turned off tomorrow, ending the steady stream of messages I've received from family and friends this year. I send one final message tonight from the growing pile of boxes and luggage at Base Camp Marietta:

Tomorrow morning we will start the trek home. Thanks for your encouragement and support. I hope that, if you ever get a chance to follow a dream like this, you'll do it. Everything worked out even better than I could have hoped. Not only was the education fun and my future path an interesting one, but I also got another chance to be part of something that I thought was only in my past.

And so this part of the adventure finally comes to an end. After one last night in what has become our vacation home, Linda and I finish packing, clean up for the next tenants, and drive home. Gary and I return the next day to load my belongings.

When I graduated from college in 1968, my brother Scott and I loaded my things into my new Firebird, and I left for a new future. Today, my son Gary and I—dubbed "two Brownsteins and a truck" by our friend Joyce—do much the same thing. After we finish loading, we settle back for the drive home, as Marietta and its friendly people shrink in our rearview mirror.

EPILOGUE

I had three weeks off before clinical rotations and used some of the time just to reintegrate myself into home life. While I had been home most weekends during the year away, I had come to consider my sparsely furnished apartment as my personal space. Now I was back in a house that seemed strangely full, even without me. Linda and I eventually put some household items into storage to give me some physical and psychic room to fit back in.

The curtain had come down on one part of the adventure, but my clinical rotations lay just ahead. It wasn't long before that experience developed its own rhythm. I would show up at a clinical site totally unfamiliar with the people working there or exactly what they did. For the first week or two, I would feel that I was learning a lot but not really contributing. Fortunately everyone—including the patients—knew that I was student PA and cut me some slack. Generally around the midpoint of the rotation, I would start to feel that, every now and then, I could contribute. Sometimes that might be by picking up subtle clues as to the patient's underlying condition, or maybe just by showing some empathy. Then it was time to move on to the next site and experience the cycle all over again.

It was a little strange being a novice again, especially after a lifetime of jobs where each position had more or less provided me with the credentials for the next. Fortunately I was living in the time of portable electronics. I carried a medical dictionary application, another to decode medical mnemonics, and a third to help with drug dosing.

My walking reference library at least cut down on my steady stream of questions, which my preceptors were universally helpful in answering. They also asked me questions, a practice called "pimping" in medical-education parlance. I was expected to have an accurate response on the spot or else research the question and provide a better answer the next day. The books I never got to use in class began to get broken in, and I got an introduction to what lifelong education really means in the medical world.

Probably my hardest lesson was accepting the fact that now I was actually qualified to help someone. I always had the option to go running to my preceptor, and, in any case, he would see every patient when I was through. But the patient had told me his or her story, I had performed my examination, and now they wanted my action plan. As time went by, I developed the confidence to share it.

I discovered that it was an advantage being an older student clinician. I was often older than my patients, or at least close enough in age to develop a rapport fairly easily. Talking to people turns out to be a readily transferable skill, even from a lifetime of nonmedical jobs. If anything, patients may have overestimated my knowledge because of my receding salt-and-pepper hair. I seldom did.

I spent the first ten weeks of my clinical year in an inner-city family practice with Dr. Michael Alexander. His office staff and patients openly admired him, and his dual background as a pharmacist and physician made him an excellent preceptor for someone just starting out in medicine.

"Dr. A's" patience and sense of humor were especially helpful as I made the transition from medical student to student clinician. Besides office visits, we also made frequent rounds at several local nursing homes, where Dr. A's lighthearted manner made him a welcome visitor, as well as an effective health-care provider. I took his lessons to heart, and I still try to get every patient to smile, regardless of whatever else might be going on in their lives.

Even with my good air-powered stethoscope, I had trouble hearing some heart sounds Dr. A could pick up with his electronic one, and so he loaned me one of his. I was very careful with it, and we pretended that he had loaned me his car. I periodically thanked "Dad" for use of his "Jaguar" as I carefully placed the stethoscope back in his desk drawer each evening.

While many family practitioners no longer perform office procedures, Dr. A gave me a chance to do some, referring to it as his "medical-student special." His patients were salt-of-the-earth people, many financially strapped, and they often brought in homemade pastries and garden-grown vegetables to share with us.

Next came my emergency-medicine rotation, where, for five weeks, I worked in the emergency department at Madison County Hospital. That's also the hospital where my squad brings most of its patients. I thought I could sense some pride in my fellow medics when they saw that it was one of their own wearing the short, white coat.

Most of my ER preceptors were good teachers, and Drs. Rivera and Sherman were two of the best. Dr. Rivera taught me how to begin developing a plan as soon as I laid eyes on a new patient. I also gained confidence in my suturing skills, along with a healthy appreciation for the importance of nurses and technicians.

At one point, I told Dr. Rivera about my difficulties using an ophthalmoscope. His reply: "I didn't figure out how to use that darned thing until I was five years out of medical school." I felt much better after that.

Most of our cases were routine lacerations and colds, but we also had our share of heart attacks and cardiac arrests. Arrests, in particular, can be frenetic affairs as people execute time-critical tasks and grab for supplies in very close quarters. One afternoon in the ER, I watched Dr. Sherman direct a cardiac arrest so calmly that he inspired tranquility and professionalism in his team. It's an example I've tried to follow ever since.

My preceptor for obstetrics and gynecology looked vaguely familiar. After spending some time comparing our lives, he turned out to be a fellow parent on the sidelines at Daniel's long-ago childhood soccer games. Working with Dr. Richards, I participated in some deliveries and watched as he performed a number of innovative surgical procedures. And any concerns I might have had about breast and vaginal examinations faded after several weeks of performing physicals under his guidance.

As summer turned to fall, I got my first taste of hospital internal medicine, working with Paul Sears, a veteran physician assistant. We also saw patients in nursing homes and in the office. I got more opportunities to perform in-office surgical procedures, as well as a chance to see my first solo patient.

One afternoon, as we performed rounds in a local nursing home, Paul told me that the next patient was "all yours." He would wait at the nurses' station until I came back from the patient's room to tell him what "we" were going to do. With some nervousness, I walked in to find a sixty-year-old disabled woman complaining of symptoms of what sounded like a urinary tract infection. I returned to Paul, telling him that I would like to order a urinalysis and start a standard antibiotic.

"OK," he said, with no sign of concern. "She's your patient."

The urine culture came back on Friday, and I changed the antibiotic to one that was better suited to the infection. Then I agonized all weekend about how I might have misread the culture results. I did online research and left several phone messages for Paul, who didn't return any of them. On Monday, he told me that he had been watching over my shoulder the whole time and that I had done everything right. He hadn't returned my calls because he wanted me to have the experience of worrying about a patient. Mission accomplished, Paul.

For my cardiology rotation, I worked with a physician who did it all: office patients, in-office cardiac testing, cardiac catheterizations, placing stents to relieve coronary blockages, and pacemaker implants. To me, cardiology was a unique blend of patient personalities; critical body systems; fluid flow; pump performance; electronics; chemistry; and cleverly designed, minimally invasive procedures.

I enjoyed my time in my preceptor's practice, but I could tell that he really didn't like the work. He would often remark, "Welcome to my world," with a sour tone in his voice. A few years later, he sold the practice and moved elsewhere to teach. Wherever he is now, I hope that he's happier.

As I did before each rotation, I visited the general surgeon's office a week ahead of time, mostly just to introduce myself and find out where I should show up on the first day. I would be working under the direction of Drs. Scott Jansen and John Haslett. Arriving at their office, my first exposure to Dr. Jansen was his booming voice coming from the break room. "Is that the *rocket* scientist?" he roared, referring to my aerospace engineering training.

Dr. Jansen proved to be a delightful guy and an excellent preceptor, with all of the self-confidence we seem to expect from successful surgeons. This was my first hands-on surgical experience, requiring me to be gloved and gowned on a regular basis. Fortunately the surgical support team helped me, as they did the physicians, so I never had to fight my way into my own gloves after all.

Our surgeons performed a mix of procedures, ranging from minimally invasive gallbladder removals, hernia repairs, and colonoscopies to more extensive procedures, such as mastectomies and major abdominal surgeries. Dr. Jansen had given me the name of a good surgical reference book on my first day, and I quickly got a copy. I was expected to read up on each procedure ahead of time, assist with suturing, and operate an internal TV camera for minimally invasive procedures. Even now, I can hear Dr. Jansen's generally good-natured exclamation of "you're *killing* me here!" if one of my sutures failed to hold or if I took too long with a task.

Once our patient was sedated, conversation in the surgical suite took on a life of its own. The surgeon would pause to highlight interesting anatomical features and surgical techniques. When there wasn't any technical information to share, he would talk informally with the staff, or we would listen to music CDs playing through speakers in the room. While there could be tense and frustrating moments, most of the conversation was light, and time passed quickly, even during long procedures.

An anesthesiologist located himself at the patient's head, separated from the rest of us by a sterile barrier. We worked with several different anesthesiologists during my stay. One in particular was a consummate storyteller, capable of holding our attention almost indefinitely with his humorous first-person stories. Even after several hours of standing in one spot, I would often be disappointed if he hadn't finished a story by the time the procedure was over.

I also got to see office patients during the rotation, generally going in first for my assessment and then again with the surgeon. An obviously ill woman came in one day with her husband. Jane was in significant pain and had been unable to hold down food for some time. She also had a history of ovarian cancer. After listening to her story and examining her, I recommended that she be admitted to the hospital, fearing that the cancer may have spread.

Eventually I took part in Jane's surgery and, over the next few weeks, followed her progress. For a time, it looked like she was improving, but then she faded. I was there the day she died. I have had many other patients die since, but I will never forget Jane.

I thoroughly enjoyed my surgical rotation. Surgery has the advantage of sometimes being able to cure a condition, rather than just trying to manage it. However, I came to realize that I preferred working with conscious patients and began thinking about a career in internal medicine.

I took a two-week break in the middle of my surgical rotation to join Dr. A and a local church group on a medical mission to Belize. We lived in a small compound and took bumpy day trips over roads that were little more than dirt paths to remote villages. We would invariably be met by crowds of villagers and would arrange for a local teenager to translate between the local Mayan dialect and English.

We also made stops in the countryside, including one at a small farm where we treated an old woman with pneumonia. We returned a few days later to find our patient feeling much better. Her daughter proudly showed us an arbor with a small solar panel mounted on its roof. The panel charged a car battery that powered the single light bulb on the ceiling of their one-room home.

During my time on the mission, I worked with a medical resident who had graduated from the same school that employed Dr. S, my organizationally-challenged anatomy instructor. I asked the resident if he knew him. "Oh yes!" he replied. "That guy caused more people to flunk out of gross anatomy, especially his section on the pelvis and peritoneum!" I guess I was almost in some pretty good company.

My pediatrics rotation was at a large children's hospital, along with a hundred or so other students from medical, pharmacy, and nursing programs. We worked in teams of about ten, and I missed the one-on-one mentoring of my other rotations. I was the only PA student in the hospital, and my attending physician wasn't exactly sure where I fit in. That made two of us.

I was given three children to care for each day, which usually took about ninety minutes. I spent the rest of the day attending lectures with the medical students, checking on my young charges again in the afternoon, and working on my thesis.

My psychiatric rotation followed, where I spent half my time in the hospital and half in a local community health clinic. For the hospital portion, I sat in on sessions with my preceptor, observed patients in the hospital's lockdown area and, on one occasion, attended a commitment hearing at the local courthouse.

Like many people of my generation, I had come to think of psychiatry as the "talking cure," necessitating many years of analysis to uncover and resolve deep-seated issues. Now I was seeing even psychotic patients helped, though certainly not cured, after just a few days on the right medications. While long-term care would still be necessary, patients generally were kept in lockdown for only a few days.

One patient we saw in lockdown was a forty-year-old man who had decided that the woman living in the apartment above his was the devil. He could even hear her "scuttling" around on what he surmised were "cloven hooves." He had sexual feelings for her, and, when they surfaced, he would "smite" himself by forcing himself to read the Bible for extended periods. Eventually he heard a voice telling him to cut off his hair and throw away all his worldly possessions. He was found by police in the middle of the night, loudly throwing his furniture in the dumpster, wild-eyed, and with a most uneven haircut.

With medications, he calmed down over the next few days. He started talking to the other patients and exercising on a treadmill. He also began to realize that his behavior had been bizarre. I last saw him the day he was transferred to another facility. Other than the haircut, he looked and acted like a normal guy.

EPILOGUE

I spent the community health-clinic portion of the rotation with a different psychiatrist. Outpatients would come to talk with him for an hour, and he would adjust their medications as needed. I came to appreciate how important this portion of the community safety net really is.

My preceptor was from Egypt, and he had started out in family practice in the Middle East, later deciding to come to the United States to study psychiatry. Before he could apply for training, he first had to spend several years studying on his own to pass the demanding series of exams needed to become an American medical doctor.

American medical students take the same tests, but, in their case, the exams are synchronized with the rest of their training. For my preceptor to pass the first few tests, he had to bone up on organic chemistry and other medical-school prerequisites, knowledge of which tends to fade with time. It gave me an appreciation for what foreign physicians are willing to go through to practice here.

Spring began with a return to surgery, this time in a large orthopedic practice. Our patients underwent back surgeries, joint replacements, and hand repairs. For joint replacements, we would dress in surgical gowns and astronaut-like transparent helmets to protect ourselves from flying bone marrow. We sat down for hand surgeries, in one case reconnecting a tendon that had been severed by broken glass.

Much of the rotation was spent in spine surgeries, working with a surgeon and his PA. They were both interested in training new practitioners. We would assemble in a conference room early on Friday mornings, where a group of physicians would discuss their cases. Everyone, including me, was expected to participate and freely admit what he or she didn't know. I thought it was a very effective problem-solving environment.

My rotations ended where they began, with a final five weeks of family practice at Dr. A's office. My return to the fold took place on my sixtieth birthday, which the staff celebrated with me. I enjoyed seeing some of the same patients again. One gentleman had been started on antidepressants the summer before and now returned in much better spirits. An ill, sickly looking fellow had been started on dronabinol, an ingredient in marijuana that causes the munchies. His appetite had quickly returned, and now he was back to his normal weight.

The staff took me out to lunch on my last day, and Dr. A gave me a parting gift. It was the Jaguar, the electronic stethoscope he had been loaning me. I was touched by his generosity and only wished his practice was large enough for me to find a permanent place in it.

Between rotations, I returned to campus for our callback days, driving past my old apartment, now in new hands. Most of us out-of-towners would come back the night before to socialize with those who had stayed behind.

After our last rotation, we became the old second years, spending two final weeks on campus before graduation. Out-of-towners were put up in a dorm that proved to be a noisy place when our local classmates stopped by to socialize. By day, we worked with the faculty, drilling for our upcoming boards and defending our theses. By night, we socialized and reacquainted ourselves with life in Marietta.

Finally, one hot summer day, we dressed in caps and gowns and graduated. The rest of that weekend involved a final class party and the marriage of one of our classmates. Then the class of 2006 disbanded for the last time.

After graduation, our class scattered across the country to start new careers. Stan eventually went to Afghanistan as an army PA, served in combat, and returned home safely. Drew got a job in my old emergency room at St. Ann's in Westerville. And my medic-school classmate Fred moved to Colorado, where he practices psychiatry. Two Marietta posters went up in my office, and they are still there today. One is the view I saw every morning, walking down the Fourth Street hill to class. The second is a cartoon map of the campus, autographed by classmates and teachers.

I joined a cardiology practice in Columbus as the second of two PAs working for Dr. Manmohan Katapadi, referred to as "Dr. K." Fortunately, I didn't have to use an ophthalmoscope in my job. I did, however, need a great many of the drugs we labored to learn in school. And, after my days with Dr. Waller, I gladly accepted help from pharmacists and nurses who often labor behind the scenes to help keep patients safe.

So there I was, sixty years old, wearing a long white coat, and being trained by Lisa, a much more experienced PA in her mid-twenties. Much of our work was at Ohio State University Hospital East, a round tower of a building in the inner city of Columbus. The patients and staff there are a mixing pot of races, nationalities, and socioeconomic statuses. You will hear doctors, nurses, janitors, and patients talking in Russian, Arabic, and other languages. Working there was physically disorienting at first, because its pie-shaped rooms and stairwells without right angles made me dizzy, and sometimes even a little nauseous.

I'm not sure that the hospital staff knew what to make of me when I arrived. My age and long coat belied an experience that I really didn't have. A neurosurgeon called me "sir" on my first day. Nurses would ask me questions that I couldn't yet answer. Some people even went out of their way to call me "Doctor Brownstein." After repeatedly telling them I was a PA, I eventually trained them to just call me Barry. And they do.

There was a lot to learn, and the staff at OSU East was very helpful. As time went on, I picked up more knowledge and became more confident in my skills. My cell phone was my lifeline, and I called Lisa and Dr. K with questions many times each day. I was encouraged to follow my own initiative, and I did, though sometimes things could go awry.

One patient was having brief episodes of a specific arrhythmia. The usual drug of choice for that is amiodarone, and it's often given via intravenous line. I ordered the proper dose, and the staff scrambled to move the patient to a floor capable of managing an IV drip medication. When I told Dr. K what I had done, I learned that, though my dose was acceptable, giving the patient the drug as one tablet twice a day would have been a better choice.

I learned from these experiences and, over time, developed a set of responses that could be scaled to the situation. I learned nuances as well, such as taking advantage of a drug's secondary effects to better match a treatment with a given patient's needs. After months of looking at telemetry traces, I got better at interpreting heart rhythms.

I was surprised when physicians started asking for my advice. I began to recognize that everyone around me was learning in more or less the same way. Regardless of our titles, we sometimes needed to ask for advice. My phone contains several critical applications that I use constantly. Hardly a day goes by that I don't wish I were half as smart as my smart phone.

Because no two situations are the same, in the end, we often have to take our best shot in the patient's interest. I sometimes refer to that as "operating in EMS mode," because, on an emergency scene, what you have with you is all you have; what you and your crew know is all you know; and now is the time you must act. You get better at this over time.

My patients are the salt of the earth; if you ask them a question, generally you will get a straight answer. Some become like family. One is a woman just a few months older than I am and bed-bound, at least partially by choice. We have a standing challenge that I will buy her some new earrings if she will sit up for at least a few hours each day. Until he passed away, another patient came dressed in a winter coat that looked like part of a monkey costume. He also brought along little boxes of shelf-stable tuna salad to eat on his travels. And still a third uses her beautiful voice to entertain fellow patients in our waiting room.

Over the years, I've developed relationships with our patients. I see them in the office every few months, and I follow them daily when they're in the hospital. I encourage some to stop smoking, others to watch their salt and water consumption, and still others to exercise. I console others who lose functionality, mates, or children.

My parents moved to town after I had been with the practice for a few years. Both were then in their late eighties and had cardiac issues. I could think of no better place for them to be seen than by our practice. And, when they needed hospitalization, I had them brought to OSU East, where my coworkers treated them like royalty.

My mother's health slowly faltered. Dr. K sent her for heart surgery at the Cleveland Clinic, where I was able to interact with her care team. She was transferred to a long-term acute-care facility in Columbus, where our practice took care of her and the attending hospitalist gave me access to her medical chart. When she finally returned home, I managed her medications and referred her to various providers.

Nearly four years later, Mom was readmitted to our hospital in Dr. K's care. I saw her daily on rounds, advocated for her, and discussed test results with Dr. K. I did not take part in her direct care because it was best that unrelated practitioners take over.

In the end, it was Mom's time to leave us. My brother, sister-in-law, and I stood watch at her bedside. She went softly and peacefully about six weeks shy of her and Dad's seventieth wedding anniversary. It had been a blessing and an honor to take care of her. The woman who played such an important role in my education had taught me some final lessons.

Running from office to office and hospital to hospital can make for a grueling job, especially for someone now old enough to get Medicare himself—if he wasn't still working twelve hour days. Probably not so surprising, my job has many of the same frustrations as any other. What makes it so different for me are those special everyday moments when I know exactly why I'm here doing this.

It might be a condition that I first suspect and then go on to diagnose and treat; or the patient who returns to say that she feels better; or the satisfaction of putting a patient and his or her family at ease; or the chance to help train someone just starting out in their career. But, just as it was nine decades ago with my grandfather's tuberculosis, there are still a lot of conditions we can't fix. Sometimes I have to be satisfied with just making a connection with someone whose days are numbered. After all, so are mine.

3 Unit crew, Madison County EMS today: From left: me, Lt. Carolyn Anderson, Justin Whitehead, Josh Carney. Andrew Scordato is behind the camera.

I still ride two shifts each month as a paramedic with the Madison County Emergency Medical District. EMS will always be in my blood. Even off duty, whenever an ambulance speeds by with lights and siren on, I can picture the crew at their positions, wondering what they're going to find. Besides camaraderie, ice cream, and the occasional adrenaline rush, life in EMS is always a constant reminder of the importance of teamwork.

Many of my old EMS crewmates have moved on to careers elsewhere, and it's always special to run into them. Several have gone on to more advanced training, and I'm happy for any role I may have had in demonstrating that advancing age is not incompatible with education. Lieutenant Carla Blazier has retired and is now a registered nurse, along with Greg Dean and Jake Gibson. Matt Paulus and Scott Woolf, the two medics who invented our word-of-the-night game, are also nurses, with Matt having gone on to become a nurse practitioner.

At Marietta College, others have followed our trail since the class of 2006. I return to campus each year to help in the selection of new students and also give a guest lecture in clinical medicine. The drive to campus always brings back memories as I pass the places we lived, studied, and relaxed. And looking out from the lectern at the mostly young faces of those who have followed us, I envy them their journey and fondly remember my time in their shoes.

Thankfully my family continues to thrive. Linda and I recently celebrated our forty-fourth anniversary. Gary continues to work as a project-management consultant. Katie and Tom now have three children; our grandson Patrick now has two younger brothers. Noah was born shortly after I graduated and Liam joined them two years ago. Daniel moved to South Carolina, where he met Pam. They were married a few years ago on his mom's birthday and now are the parents of Sanford Wolfe, our fourth grandchild.

We're fortunate that my father and Linda's mother are still with us. The twenty-nine-year-old father who long ago chased the three-year-old version of me through a field of airplanes recently turned ninety-two. Hanging on a wall in his apartment is a plaque of college graduates that he and Mom helped over the years. It now includes a picture of me.

With Dad, reunited with a P-51.

Sometimes in life we get the chance to come full circle. After graduation, my father and I visited a local air show and, sixty years later, reprised our walk through a field of P-51s. This time, however, neither of us was short enough to clamber beneath their wings.

Another déjà vu moment is taking place today at St. Ann's Hospital. This is where I started my medical career twenty-six years ago as an emergency-room volunteer. Where we took patients during my time with the Minerva Park Volunteer Fire Department. Where my broken wrist was set. Where my children were treated for assorted teenage emergencies. Where Linda had her surgery while I was in PA school. And where our grandson Liam was born.

Tonight, though, I'm not a volunteer, an EMT, a patient, a husband, a parent, or a grandfather holding his newborn grandson for the first time. I'm a physician assistant with privileges here, wearing my long white coat as I pass a display of the faded pictures of nurses I used to work with as a volunteer. I'm on my way to meet a patient for a cardiac consultation. Life has moved on in mysterious ways.

I don't know what will happen next in my life. I would like to think that I'm still open to new adventures. And my old short-sleeve, blue-and-white striped freshman shirt is still in my closet, waiting for whatever the next one turns out to be.

Our next generation. From left: Patrick, Sanford Wolfe, me, Liam, Linda, and Noah.

Made in the USA
Lexington, KY
01 May 2013